The Rhine

Great Rivers of the World

The Rhine

Goronwy Rees

G. P. PUTNAM'S SONS
NEW YORK

FIRST AMERICAN EDITION 1967

© 1967 by Goronwy Rees

Library of Congress Catalog
Card Number: 67-23013

PRINTED IN THE UNITED STATES OF AMERICA

To Jenny and Lucy

Contents

Illustrations

Following page 96

Acknowledgements

The author and publishers are grateful to the following for providing illustrations: Aart Fotograaf Klein, figure 49; Aerofilms,
figures 5, 7, 38 and 47; Bavaria-Verlag, figures 2 and 3;
Bildarchiv Foto Marburg, figures 6, 15, 17, 18, 27 and 37;
Black Star Pictures, figures 8 and 39; British Museum, figures
16 and 23; Camera Press, figures 13, 31, 35 and 36; Douglas
Dickins, figures 4, 14 and 22; Fox Photos, figure 30; John
Freeman, figures 29 and 43; German Tourist Information Bureau,
figures 9, 11, 12, 19, 25, 34, 40 and 41; Giraudon, figures 20 and
48; Keystone, figure 33; Mansell Collection, figures 10, 21, 24, 26,
32 and 45; Walter Moog, figures 42 and 46; Rheinisches
Bildarchiv, figure 28; Ullstein Bilderdienst, figure 1; Roger
Viollet, figure 44.

Map drawn Audrey Frew

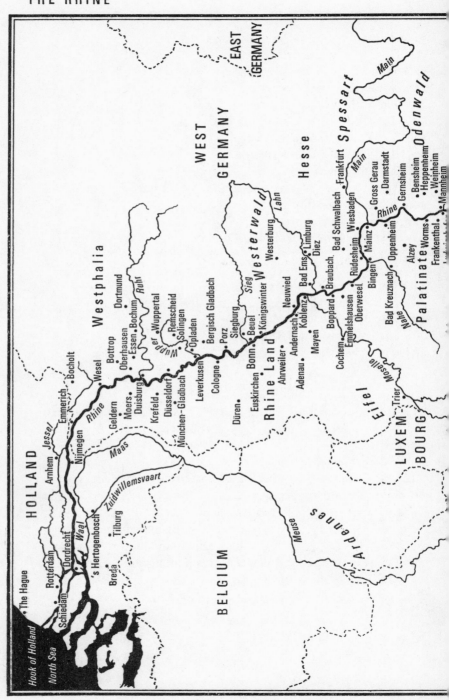

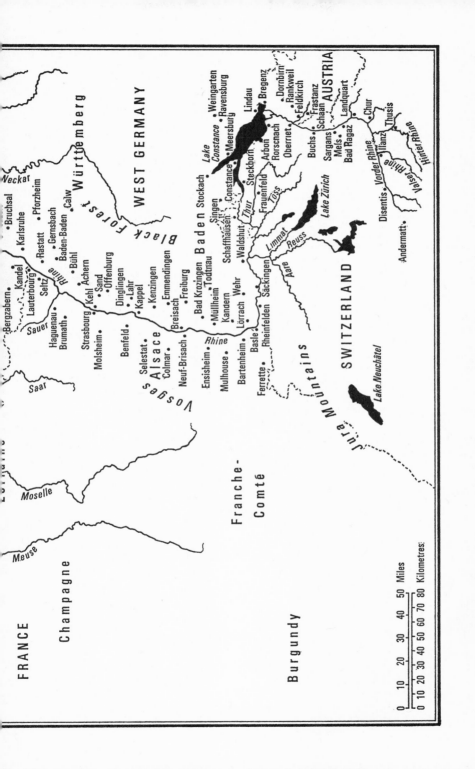

1 The River

The Rhine is the greatest of all Europe's rivers. There are others which have played as great a part in the lives of those who inhabit its banks, the Thames, the Seine, the Danube, the Volga, and there are others which have their own particular beauties and their own particular historical significance. But there are none which have played so vital a part in the development of modern Europe, whose fate has been so inextricably bound up with the fate of Europe as a whole, or which have been the cause in history of such incessant dissension and conflict. In every century great armies have fought for possession of its banks, its bridges, its crossings, its cities, in a way that no other river has ever been fought for; but perhaps today, after the greatest of all the wars in which the Rhine has played a part, the time has come when it will be possible to say at last of the Rhine what Lincoln said of the Mississippi, that 'the father of waters rolls unvexed to the sea'.

In his book on the Rhine, written in 1908, before two great wars seemed to have shattered irretrievably the unity of Europe, the great geographer and geo-politician, Sir Halford Mackinder, wrote, 'When the Roman organization broke down, and the Frankish or German dominion spread during several centuries from the borders of Bohemia to the border of Brittany, it must have appeared that so far from being a national frontier, the Rhine and the Rhine basin were destined to be the metropolitan features of a united northern Europe, composed of the whole of the unbroken plain which extends from the Pyrenees by the oceanic shores to the Baltic.' What seemed possible then has been disproved by fifteen centuries of conflict, but today it seems that it may be possible once more, and if that is so it is also possible that the future of the Rhine may be even greater than its past.

The significance of the Rhine in the life of Europe arises both from its geographical conformation and from the historical development of the peoples who inhabit its banks; what gives the Rhine its peculiar fascination in that these two factors have been in perpetual conflict. Geographically, the river has the natural function of uniting the heartland of Europe, deep in the great Alpine masses that divide the north from the south, with its northern plain and the Atlantic; it is a waterway which connects the whole of northern Europe, and brings sea-going traffic deep into the continent as far as Mannheim, five hundred miles from the sea. Moreover, from its Alpine sources, it provides, by way of the Danube and the Po, connections with Vienna in the east and Rome in the south. It is natural that Charlemagne's dream of a European empire should have as its two capitals Rome on the Tiber and Aachen near the Rhine, the two poles between which the great waterway of the Rhine provides an indispensable link. It was not entirely poetic fancy or classical nostalgia that made Hölderlin, sitting at the sources of the Rhine, 'amid the dark ivy, at the gate of the forest, as the golden afternoon touched its springs' turn his thoughts, not to the north, but to the south as far as the Morea and Asia, as he heard the thunder of its mountain torrents;

> 'Die Stimme wars der edelsten der Ströme,
> Des freigeborenen Rheins.'

> (It was the voice of the noblest of all rivers,
> The freeborn Rhine.)

On its 800–mile course from the Alps to the sea, the river drains an area of 76,000 square miles, carrying the icy waters of its mountain sources through narrow gorges, broad valleys and wide plains, past great cities, cathedrals, castles, ruins that bear the marks of over two thousand years of history; at the same time, it is a great modern commercial waterway, linked by canal with the Marne, the Rhône and the Danube and carrying to Rotterdam, by giant barges and sea-going ships, a fifth of Germany's overseas trade.

Its remotest sources rise in the heart of the Alps, in the canton of the Grisons, or Graubünden, where from mountain peaks of over 12,000 feet some 2,000 glacier-fed torrents gather to form two main head streams, the Vorder Rhein and the Hinter Rhein, which flow north-eastwards to join near the little Alpine town of Chur and thence northward to Lake Constance. From the lake it turns west to Basle and just short of the German-Swiss frontier is joined by its first great tributary, the Aar, bringing with it the waters of the northern range of the Alps. From the Lake of Constance, which the Germans call the Bodensee, to Basle, the Rhine is still an Alpine river, falling from 1,200 feet to 800 feet above sea level in thirty-five miles, its waters swollen in June and July by the melting of the mountain snows. At Schaffhausen, the river falls in a spectacular cascade of over a hundred feet which has been harnessed to provide electric power.

At Basle the Rhine ceases to be a Swiss or an Alpine river, and entering Germany loses something of the cold, green freshness which it draws from the alpine snows and glaciers. The Germans indeed are apt to look on the Swiss Rhine as almost a different river from their own, from which it is so sharply distinguished geographically, historically and politically that it seems to belong to another world.

When the Germans speak of the Upper Rhine, they do not mean the Rhine of the Alps, but the Rhine on its course through the wide gentle valley, the *Tiefebene*, which extends for 180 miles between Basle and Bingen. On the west it is enclosed by the Vosges and Hardt mountains and on the east by the Black Forest and the Odenwald; as it meanders through the valley, its tributary, the Ill, flows parallel with it on the west; from the east, it is joined, at Mannheim and Mainz, by its two beautiful tributaries of the Neckar and the Main. Sometimes these valleys, and the main stream itself, are suffused in a golden gentle light that encloses them like the skin of a fruit; they breathe the enchanted air of Hölderlin's poem to the Neckar;

Auf ihren Gipfeln löste des Himmels Luft
Mir oft der Knechtschaft Schmerzen;
und aus dem Tal

Wie Leben aus dem Freudebecher
Glanzte die Blaüliche Silberwelle.

Der Berge Quellen eilten hinab zu dir,
Mit ihnen auch mein Herz, und du nahmst uns mit
Zum stillerhabenen Rhein, zu seinen
Städten herunter und lustgen Inseln.

(Often on your peaks the air of Heaven
Healed the pains of servitude; and in the valley,
As if poured from life's cup of joy
Your blue-veined waves of silver danced.

The mountain streams hurried down to you,
And with them my heart, and you took
    us with you
To the calm and noble Rhine, down
To its cities and its happy islands.)

The valley, known as the Rift valley, or *Graben*, ends at Mainz, where the river takes a sharp turn west to Bingen. Vineyards rise steeply on its northern bank, and the Taunus mountains gradually press closer until at Bingen the river enters the great eighty-mile gorge of the Middle Rhine from Bingen to Bonn. Here the Rhine cuts straight through the high plateau of the Taunus and Hünsruck ranges, which rise precipitously from its banks, their heights crowned by castles which look down into the green waters of the river as they flow strongly and deeply in their narrow channel through the mountains. These form the steep south-eastern end of a broad upland plateau of hard, dark slatelike rock, bare, undulating and desolate. The powerful current of the river at places fills the whole width of the valley, and terraces and vineyards contain the steep slopes of the gorge which at some points, as at the Lorelei, tower like a precipice over the river running nearly eighty feet deep at their feet. When sunlight fills the gorge, it is as if it were brimming over with some golden liquid and even today it would not be difficult to catch an echo of the Lorelei's mysterious and seductive song.

At Mannheim the river has undergone another important change; for between there and the sea, in spite of the navigational hazards of the gorge, it becomes navigable to ocean-going ships, and this has made Mannheim the largest inland port in Europe. Near Coblenz, the uplands fall away for a short distance and the valley widens to receive, on the river's right bank, the two tributaries of the Moselle and the Lahn; from the Moselle and its tributary the Saar, the Rhine receives the waters of the area between the Vosges and the Ardennes. At Coblenz the valley narrows again until, a short way below Bonn, the Rhine finds its northern exit from the mountains into the plain which divides it from the sea.

Bonn, at the southern edge of the plain, marks the beginning of the Lower Rhine; the hills fall away as the river enters the Cologne 'gulf', a wide deltaic plain, until, between Aachen on the west and Essen on the east, they are separated by a hundred miles. Below Cologne the river receives from its right bank the tributaries of the Ruhr and the Lippe, which drain an area which contains the greatest industrial concentration in Europe. From here onwards to the sea the Rhine becomes a slow, broad, sluggish river as it crosses the great northern plain which includes the whole of French Flanders, northern Belgium, and all of Holland and stretches through northern Germany beyond Berlin to Russia and the Urals. Its river bed is formed of deltaic deposits left behind by more ancient rivers and wide terraces mark former river levels. Beyond Emmerich, where the Rhine turns west to leave Germany and enter Holland, dykes become necessary and the river breaks up into main streams, the Lek, and the Waal, which carries two-thirds of its waters; the Waal itself merges with the Meuse in the many channels of the delta by which they both find the sea through the Hollandsch Diep.

No end could be less like its beginning; the icy torrents of the Alps are wholly unrecognizable in the sandy sluggish waters of the mouths of the Rhine as they reach the sea. Between these two extremes the river has undergone a number of changes which gives it an incomparable variety and interest. From its source down to Strasbourg the river is fed only by the Alpine water of

snows and glaciers so that its level varies greatly, at its lowest in
January and at flood in June and July. With the entry of the Neckar
its flow becomes more regular, as the snow waters melt earlier,
while the whole of the Middle and Lower Rhine basin receives
more rain than snow water and the level of the river varies little
except in exceptional seasons of summer drought or of heavy and
persistent rains.

But despite the variety of the Rhine, both in its natural and its
man-made features, the river and its tributaries remain essentially
the single central axis of a system of water communications which
is one of the permanent factors making for the unity of northern
Europe. Moreover, it is part of an even larger network which
connects northern with eastern Europe by way of the Danube,
and with the south and the Mediterranean by the passes of the
Alps in which the Rhine has its source. In the Dark and Middle
Ages especially, when the Roman road system had disintegrated,
this river network was one of the factors which helped to maintain the unity of European civilization and to provide the communications by which trade could flow from north to south and
from east to west.

The great northern plain into which the Rhine breaks at Bonn
is orientated towards the sea; ocean-going trade is its life blood
and the Dutch Republic at the river's mouth was a child of the
sea as Venice was. But south of the gorge through which the
river flows from Bingen to Bonn, the narrow, smiling, grape-
laden valleys of the Upper Rhine, the Neckar and the Moselle
form a landlocked world of their own; if the Rhine provides its
one great outlet to the sea, it also provides another outlet across
the passes of the Alps to the south and the east, by the Rhône to
Marseilles and by the Danube to Vienna.

Between the highlands of the Upper Rhine and the northern
plain there lies a great divide which is as sharply marked between
the physical configuration of their landscape as between the
characteristics of their peoples. It has been a natural function of
the Rhine to unite these two worlds, and through its tributaries
to connect them with even wider horizons. But geography is
made by man as much as by nature, and during two thousand

years of history it has also been a function of the Rhine to divide
peoples and cultures as much as to unite them, to be a barrier and
a frontier as much as a means of communication.

In modern times, it has been the fate of the Rhine to be a cause
of bitter conflict and dissension, a symbol of intense national
rivalries, and a constant danger to the peace of Europe; in particular, possession of its left bank has been the object of what
once seemed to be the irreconcilable ambitions of France and
Germany. In this form at least conflict over the Rhine has been of
comparatively recent origin, largely because Germany herself
was a newcomer among the nation states of Europe and, until
she was united, did not offer any threat to French security. The
soldiers' songs inspired by the Rhine are an expression of the
growing nationalism, belligerent and aggressive, of the European
states after the outbreak of the French revolution; the greatest of
all marching songs, the Marseillaise itself, was written by Rouget
de L'Isle at Strasbourg in 1894, as the battle hymn of that army
of the Rhine to which the Directory had entrusted the task of
securing the left bank of the river as the 'natural' frontier of
France. *Die Wacht am Rhein*, with its defiant opening;

> Sie sollen ihn nicht haben
> Die freien Deutschen Rhein
> (You shall never possess it,
> The free German Rhine),

to which the German army mobilized in 1870, was written by
Johannes Becker in 1840, when the peace of Europe was suddenly
threatened by an outburst of violent nationalist agitation both in
France and in Germany. *The Watch on the Rhine* was answered by
Alfred de Musset's equally belligerent poem;

> Nous avons eu votre Rhin allemand.
> (Your German Rhine was ours.)

And even England has its own music-hall version of the river's
soldiers' songs in the opening lines of *Mademoiselle from Aimen-
tières*,

> Two German officers crossed the Rhine,
> *Parlez-vous.*

Yet though the full bitterness of Franco-German conflict did not reach its height, and produce its appalling consequences, until 1870, the idea that the Rhine constitutes a 'natural' frontier in Europe has had a long history, which goes back to the days when the Emperor Augustus fixed the eastern limit of the Roman Empire on the Rhine.

It was perhaps natural that the Romans should look on the Rhine as a frontier, a line of division, a means of defence; for Rome was essentially a road empire, whose communications ran by land and not by water. It was also a soldiers' empire, an empire of the legions, for whom a great river was a military obstacle, something to cross or to defend, not a route by which to travel. Yet the Rhine frontier established by Rome was not yet a boundary between nations, because nations in the modern sense did not yet exist. It was a frontier between civilization and barbarism, between Roman law and tribal custom, and in time it was to become also a linguistic frontier, and a religious frontier between Christianity and paganism. In the eyes of many Frenchmen it was to acquire the significance of a barrier raised by Nature herself for the defence and protection of a superior moral and intellectual order.

But viewed from the other bank, the Rhine has appeared in an entirely different perspective, as an integral and inalienable part of the patrimony of the Germanic tribes. *Rhein, deutsche Strom, nicht Deutschland's Grenze,* (The Rhine, German river, not Germany's frontier) says the inscription on the statue of Ernst Moritz Arndt at Bonn, overlooking the river. In fact, the history of the Rhine has been a perpetual conflict between the French and German conceptions of the role of the river. The Germans have conceived of the river as their own river, and the landscape through which it flows, on both banks, as a part of their land. The French have looked towards the Rhine as a moat which would defend them against invasion by peoples whom the Romans never succeeded in civilizing, and when those peoples established a united national state, and as its military and industrial strength increased, possession of the left bank of the Rhine came to seem indispensable to French security.

The conflict between these two views has persisted for centuries, and underwent many modifications before it assumed the extreme form in which it has manifested itself in the last and present centuries. Before the death of Augustus, Roman Gaul had already been extended by the addition of the two new provinces, both west of the river, of Upper and Lower Germany, the first including Strasbourg and Mainz, and the second Cologne and Aachen. After his death, the frontier was advanced east of the Rhine to include the valleys of the Neckar and the lower Main. Here, and in theWetterau, the riverless valley which stretches from Giessen on the Lahn to Frankfurt-am-Main, one may still find traces of the entrenchments, or *Pfahlgraben*, which the Romans threw up to protect their advanced settlements. From Cologne down to the sea, the frontier still follows the river along its west bank, in the Netherlands along the ancient course of the river, from which the modern Rhine has diverged considerably.

The fall of the Roman Empire in the west saw the end of the civilization of which the Rhine had been the frontier, though its monuments still survive near and on the banks of the river, at Mainz, Cologne, Trier, Aachen and elsewhere. It is significant that these towns of Roman settlement have preserved their French names, Mayence, Cologne, Trèves, Aix-la-Chapelle; it is the mark of their origin as the outposts of the empire, on the edge of the river which divided them from the fogs and mists of the barbarians.

With the decline and fall of the Roman power, the river was no defence against the tribes which swarmed out of Germany. West, to modern France, went the Rhineland tribes known as the Franks, or Freemen; south, to Italy, the Lombards; to Spain, the Visigoths. For a brief moment, in the 7th century AD it seemed as if a new empire of the west might be created out of their conquests by Charlemange, and of this empire the Rhine and the Rhine Basin would have formed the metropolitan area, for Charlemagne built palaces for himself both at Aachen and Ingelheim, near the left bank of the river. But on his death, the empire which he had briefly founded, was partitioned among his successors and divided into three parallel belts of territory.

To the west lay Carolingia, extending from the Scheldt to the Pyrénées; to the east lay the *Regnum Teutonicum*, the kingdom of the Germans, and modern German history may properly be said to begin with the settlement of Verdun; between them lay Lotharingia, the personal dominion of the Emperor Lothair I, which stretched from the mouths of the Rhine in the north through Belgium, the Rhineland and modern Lorraine to the basin of the Saône and the Rhône and thence over the Alps to take in the whole of modern Italy including Rome. In this division of Charlemagne's empire one may still find a reflection of the Imperial idea. Carolingia, out of which came modern France, and the *Regnum Teutonicum*, from which came modern Germany, were conceived as sub-divisions of an empire whose central area, under the personal rule of the Emperor, stretched between the two imperial capitals of Aachen in the north and Rome in the south.

Lotharingia, however, was a purely artificial creation, the personal domain of the Emperor; when Charlemagne's empire was finally partitioned in 887 AD, it was divided into four imperial kingdoms, Carolingia, Germany, Burgundy and Italy, and Lotharingia as an independent entity disappeared. The imperial lands south of the Alps became Italy; the basin of the Rhône became the kingdom of Burgundy. The northern remainder, lying chiefly but not wholly west of the Rhine, and consisting of the basins of the Moselle and the Meuse, passed to the kingdom of Germany. This area retained the name of Lotharingia, which became the modern Lorraine.

The partition of Verdun laid the foundation for modern European history, and is the basis of Germany's historical claim to the left bank of the Rhine. Equally, by creating the western kingdom of Carolingia, it gave birth to modern France, which has regarded itself as the inheritor of the whole of ancient Gaul, including the Rhine frontier; over a thousand years later these two competing claims to the left bank of the Rhine were still alive to disturb the peace of Europe.

But in the new Europe that was born in 887, the Rhine assumed a different significance from what it had had before. As Roman civilization decayed, it was slowly replaced by feudalism. But the new masters of Europe were not engineers like the Romans. They had neither the material resources nor the technical skill to maintain the magnificent Roman road system, and as the roads disintegrated they were replaced by rivers as a means of communication. The function of the Rhine as the natural frontier between France and Germany was taken over by the watershed between the Moselle and the Meuse, flowing north-east into the Rhine, and the Oise and the Marne flowing south-west; and the Rhine itself became a part of the new Europe's river network.

Thus in the Middle Ages the Rhine fulfilled the same function as General de Gaulle has ascribed to it today, 'Le Rhin est une rue!' (The Rhine is a road!) The German kingdom to which it belonged was itself composed of four tribal areas, each served by a river or rivers. In the north, the Saxons, occupying an area roughly corresponding to Westphalia, stretched almost to the Rhine, but their own river was the Wesel. In the east, the Bavarians extended along the Danube towards Hungary. The Alemanni or Swabians were the people of the Upper Danube and the Upper Rhine; hence Lake Constance's name of the Swabian Sea. And in Middle Germany along the river Main to the Rhine and thence to the sea, and from the Rhine up the Meuse and the Moselle were the Franks or Middle Germans.

From these tribal areas grew the relatively stable feudal states of the Middle Ages. The Alemanni of the Upper Danube and the Upper Rhine became the Swabians whose duchy included modern Alsace west of the Rhine. East of the Rhine lay the duchy of the Franks, which reached the left bank of the river at Mainz, and included territory within the Rhineland. The Germany which grew out of the partition of the Carolingian empire was a collection of feudal states bound together by the Rhine and its tributaries to the north and south and to the east and west. But it was a part of Germany's destiny, perhaps a fatal one, that no imperial capital was founded on the Rhine and the functions of the capital were divided between different cities; the Holy Roman Emperor was chosen at Frankfurt, crowned at Aachen and buried at Speyer. It is not fanciful to find a similar dispersal of function today between the cities of the German Fedral Republic, which is also largely a Rhineland state. Its political capital is at Bonn, its financial capital at Frankfurt, its industrial capital at Düsseldorf, its judical capital at Karlsruhe, and its maritime capital at Hamburg. And just as the failure to found a capital on the Rhine was a sign of the weakness of the Holy Roman Empire, so the lack of a genuine capital is a source of weakness in the Western Germany of today.

In the loosely organized political structure of the Teutonic tribes which in northern Europe became the heirs of Rome, the Franks of the Rhineland held a central position, but they were not able to found a strong and stable state which might have become the nucleus of a united Germany, predominantly orientated towards the West. This was due to divisions which were deeply rooted in the facts both of history and geography, and in these the Rhine itself had a considerable part. The Franks remained Teutonic in character, and in language, only in the valley of the Main and along the Middle Rhine. West of the river they mingled and merged with the Latinized population which lay within the frontiers of the Roman Empire, and lost their Teutonic character-istics. It is significant that the Treaty of Verdun had to be drafted in two languages because the tribes east and west of the Rhine could no longer understand each other. Thus the German king-dom was weakened at its centre and this tended to increase the contrast between its northern, or Saxon, areas and the southern territories of the Swabians and Bavarians. Moreover, as already mentioned, Lotharingia itself had no tribal basis to give it unity and cohesion; it was merely an accidental conjunction of terri-tories which had been the personal possessions of Lothair. This lack of cohesion was increased by the natural configuration of the Rhine basin; Lower Lotharingia south of the plateau which the Rhine enters at Bingen later became the Duchy of Lorraine, or Lothringen, while Upper Lotharingia, north of the mountains, became the Duchy of Brabant.

The process of subdivision which took place in the five suc-cessor duchies of Charlemagne's German kingdom continued for centuries and indeed up to the French Revolution; and it had a decisive influence both on the destiny of the Rhine and on the development of modern Europe. On Germany's eastern frontier, which for centuries was threatened by the Slavs and the Magyars, strong dynasties arose to protect them, Hapsburgs in the south, Hohenzollerns in the north, and founded stable and powerful states. In the west, however, for centuries no such threat existed, because during the Middle Ages France's energies were absorbed in her struggle with England, and there was no need to form a common defence against an internal enemy. Moreover, in Lotharingia there were no memories of a former national or tribal existence such as could be found among the Bavarians and Saxons and helped to preserve their historical identity.

The political confusion which followed the breakdown of the feudal organization of Europe was nowhere more marked than in the basin of the Rhine. Here, on the old frontier between Rome and barbarism, there grew up a bewilderingly complex and fragmented pattern of petty states, lay and ecclesiastical, which for centuries was a cause of division and dissension in Europe; but if these states were a cause of political weakness, they also helped to create an immensely varied pattern of life and culture along the Rhine, which even today is one of the charms of the river.

To all the other reasons which prevented the growth of a strong national state in the Rhine basin, one further one must be added. The Rhine was not only the frontier between Romans and Teutons, between law and custom, between civilization and barbarism; it also became the frontier between Christianity and paganism, and the boundary across which, and the road by which, the Church tried to extend its spiritual domain. Missionary efforts to the Germans were concentrated in the three bishoprics immediately west of the Rhine—Cologne, Trier and Mainz. The missionaries sailed up the Rhine to convert the Saxons and Friesians of the northern plain; from Trier, by way of Moselle, they made their way to Coblenz and up the Lahn; Mainz especially had a particularly wide ecclesiastical jurisdiction, and from there the Gospel spread north, east and south along the Main and the

Neckar and by the Wetterau as far as the sea, the Alps and Bohemia.

The missionary efforts of the early Church made the lands of the Franks west of the Rhine the centre of ecclesiastical organization for the whole of Germany; that is to say, the power of the Church was strongest precisely where political organization was weakest and most fragmented. Under such conditions, bishops and archbishops were able to transform their spiritual into a temporal power, at Utrecht, Liége, Munster, Paderborn, Cologne, Trier, Mainz, Wurzburg, Bamberg, Worms, Speyer, Strasbourg, Basle, Metz, Toul, Verdun. Ecclesiastical rule was all the more stable and permanent because it was not exposed to either of the two dangers which permanently threatened all feudal states; the failure of heirs, or the transfer of sovereignty by marriage. In the absence of a strong state to curb their pretensions, the ecclesiastical principalities endured for centuries, and the great churches and cathedrals of the Rhine basin remain today as magnificent memorials to an age in which Christ was not only saviour but king.

In two areas, however, political disunity was overcome, and both at the river's mouth and at its source strong and stable states were established. The difference in their political development again emphasizes the contrast between the south and the north of the Rhine basin. At the source of the river, the peasant communities of the Alpine valleys combined together to form the federated republic of Switzerland. At its mouth, the duchy and county of the Netherlands first came under the rule of the House of Burgundy, passed by marriage to the House of Hapsburg, and finally formed the two states of Holland and Belgium after the Dutch war of independence. Thus both Switzerland and the Netherlands were lost to the Germans of the Upper and Middle Rhine, and this again helped to prevent the emergence of a great power based upon the river. In its absence, the Middle and Upper Rhine basin remained an area of political weakness and confusion; the Rhine cities from Basle to Cologne tried but failed to maintain their independence as members of the Hanseatic League, and when the wars of religion broke out the German Rhine became the scene of a protracted and largely meaningless struggle between petty principalities.

But the wars of religion inaugurated a new era in the history of the Rhine. Freed from the burden of her struggle with England, and with her internal power firmly consolidated, France was able to turn her attention to her eastern frontier where it was her primary object to keep Germany weak and divided. Under Richelieu and Mazarin, she concentrated on maintaining and exacerbating the divisions between the states of the Rhine basin and on advancing the frontier towards the river. In the sixteenth century the bishoprics of Toul, Verdun and Metz were annexed and secularized; in the seventeenth century, under Louis XIV, Alsace was incorporated into France; the Middle Rhine basin was ravaged by Louis' wars, and Heidelberg especially suffered severely. In the eighteenth century France acquired the Duchy of Lorraine.

What the Bourbons attempted, the French Revolution completed. Mainz, which was occupied by Custine in 1792, lost in 1793, and reoccupied in 1797, became for a time a French department and in 1800 the Treaty of Lunéville made France coterminus with Roman Gaul and restored her ancient, 'natural' frontier on the Rhine. The ecclesiastical states on the left bank of the Rhine ceased to exist, their territories were reorganized as French departments and the Code Napoleon was introduced.

Napoleon's victories achieved a settlement of the Rhine question which had for centuries been the object of French policy. But his work was undone by the Congress of Vienna which decided the shape of Europe for the next fifty years. South Germany was organized into the three independent states of Bavaria, Württemberg and Baden, with Baden's frontier on the Rhine from Constance to Heidelberg. The historic lands which had once formed Lotharingia were once again divided; in the south, Lorraine and Swabian Alsace remained with France; Belgium and the Rhineland north of Heidelberg were detached, the first as an independent kingdom, the second to become a province of Prussia.

The settlement imposed in 1815 brought peace to the Rhineland for over fifty years. It seemed as if it might be disturbed in 1840, when France found herself faced by a revival of the victorious alliance of 1815, and Europe was surprised and alarmed by the violence and intensity of nationalist feelings on both sides of the Rhine. On that occasion war did not materialize, but the bitterness of feeling persisted; in 1854, *Die Wacht am Rhein* was set to the music to which the Germans marched in 1870.

In that war also the Rhine played its part. Napoleon III's ambitions to make the Rhine again a French frontier, as a counterweight to the growing power of Prussia and Italy, was exploited by Bismarck in order to ally Prussia with the south German states with which it had been at war in 1866. Bismarck tempted Napoleon's appetite with prospects of receiving, at one time, Mainz and Kaiserslautern, and at another, Saarbrücken and Trier; but in the event the Franco-Prussian war of 1870 threw France back from the river, and the acquisition of Alsace and Lorraine by the new German Empire, perhaps the greatest single mistake ever committed by Bismarck, created in France the bitter resentment and determination to have her revenge which helped to provoke the war of 1914–18.

In that war France achieved her revenge for 1870; but in French eyes the immense sacrifices she was called upon to make could only be justified if she secured the left bank of the Rhine as a guarantee of her security. The Treaty of Versailles failed to satisfy her demands; and neither the demilitarization of the left bank nor its occupation by the Allies, nor the political guarantees provided by the Treaty, or by the League of Nations, could compensate her for the loss of the Rhine frontier.

Cheated, as she felt, of her 'natural' frontier, France attempted for many years to establish an independent Rhineland; her efforts gained considerable strength from the French and Belgian occupation of the Ruhr in 1923. But by 1930 the last Allied troops had been evacuated from the Rhineland; the President of the Rhineland High Commission declared ominously; 'All that remains on the Rhine is the word that Germany has given. The future depends on how that word is kept.' France's worst fears were realized in 1936, when Hitler denounced the Rhineland clauses of the Treaty of Versailles and his troops reoccupied the demilitarized zone on the left bank. Hitler's act was a step towards war; but it is significant that public opinion outside France, and especially in Britain, regarded it as a justified assertion of sovereignty over an area, and a river, which were thought to be inalienably German.

The remilitarization of the Rhineland made it possible for Germany once again to mount an invasion of France but when, after the Allied invasion of Normandy, the German armies were forced to retreat the Rhine became a formidable barrier to the Allied advance. Failure to seize a bridgehead across the river in 1944 meant that the war was prolonged into 1945, through long months of immeasurable suffering and destruction, even though Germany's armies in the west were routed and disorganized. Behind the barrier of the Rhine, they were able to reform and refit with consequences which were to be of momentous historical importance to Europe.

During those months, the Allies continued their immensely destructive air bombardment of Germany, in which the Rhine and its cities suffered appalling damage. In that terrible air offensive, many of the Rhine's greatest treasures were lost, more priceless than all the gold of the Nibelungen. But, ironically, Allied bombing also uncovered sites which revealed undamaged remains which had been hidden for centuries. In the Council of Europe's exhibition held at Aachen in 1965 on the site of Charlemagne's palace, among other relics were to be seen jewels, rings, amulets, bracelets, harnesses that had been dug up among the ruins left by the war in the Rhineland and still testify by their beauty to the splendour of Charlemagne's dream of Europe.

The war also saw the end of a process which destroyed one of the most fruitful and productive elements in the life of the Rhine and its cities. Among the many races whose blood had been mingled and spilled on its banks, Romans, Gauls, Franks, Frenchmen, Germans, there was one other which made its own very special contribution to its history. When the Jews of the Diaspora were scattered throughout the world, they founded communities in Roman times on the Rhine at Speyer, Worms, Mainz and

Cologne and on the Moselle at Metz and Trier and during the
Middle Ages their colonies flourished under imperial protection
in all the cities of the Rhineland. Until Hitler's 'final solution',
they had formed for nearly two thousand years an integral part
of the life and culture of the river. In their cities or settlements
they left behind them memorials which provide yet another link
with the river's most ancient past, jewelled manuscripts, sculptures,
paintings in which Christ is revealed as the heir of the old dis-
pensation, gold and enamelled Trees of Jesse that show his descent
from the prophets, ritual symbols of their faith which, beaten in
gold and resplendent with jewels, ornamented the crown of a
Holy Roman Emperor.

Through the centuries the Jews of the Rhineland suffered
persecution but also enjoyed periods in which they lived under
imperial protection and, later, reaped the benefits of eighteenth
century enlightenment, and to the life of the Rhineland they
made a contribution which was immensely productive both in
the arts and sciences and in commerce and banking. And if they
looked back to centuries of history on the Rhine, they also helped
to inaugurate a future that would shake the world; it was in a
Rhineland paper, the *Neue Rheinische Zeitung*, in the revolutionary year of 1848 that the young Karl Marx wrote his first appeals
for a violent overthrow of existing institutions, and it was in the
Rhineland that the ancestors of Freud were born.

All this was brought to an end during the last war, when the
Jews of the Rhineland were deported from the homes of their
ancestors to feed the gas chambers of Auschwitz and Sachsen-
hausen. Yet a visitor to the Rhineland in 1945 might have been
excused for thinking that the destruction which had fallen on the
Jews was no more final and complete than that which had
devasted the life of the river as a whole, as if Jew and Gentile had
perished together in a common holocaust. Its cities lay in ruins,
its industries were destroyed, its trade and commerce at an end
and its people defeated and without hope; only the river, with its
torrents and gorges, its green depths of water, its vineyard covered
hills, continued to flow as before and provide a waterway along
which life could revive again.

If one had asked why the Rhineland had suffered such a fate, as if visited by fire from Heaven, a part at least of the answer would have to be found in the hatreds and enmities which have divided the peoples who lived on the banks of the great river; and if today life has returned to the river, with a prosperity and in an abundance which exceeds anything that has preceded it, it is because, in the years following the war, the two great nations which it has divided for so long have found a means to bury their ancient emnity, so that once again the Rhine can play the part it was designed to play in the dream of Charlemagne, as the freely flowing river which forms the central axis of a united Europe.

In this new Europe the Rhine can claim a heritage, both of history and of legend, such as no other European river possesses, and it is an essential part of its fascination and charm that its waters, at every stage of their course, seem to reflect so many images of the past. The Rhine flows through time as well as space; and for all the richness and complexity of the commercial life which crowds its banks and its waters today, it still has the power to bewitch and enchant which inspired Heine's poem to the Lorelei;

> Ich weiss nicht was soll es bedeuten
> Das ich so traurig bin;
> Ein Märchen von alten Zeiten,
> Es kommt mir nicht aus dem Sinn.

> (I can't think what it is
> That has made me so melancholy;
> It's an ancient legend,
> That I can't get out of my mind.)

2   The Swiss Rhine

THE SOURCES

On its course from the Alps to the sea, the Rhine flows through so
varied a landscape, such a diversity of peoples, so many cities, so
complex a web of cultures, that at times it is difficult to remember
that it is a single and continuous stream, which imposes its own
unity on the lands through which it flows. Indeed, it is its variety,
and the depth of the historical memories with which it is associated, rather than mere length, which make the Rhine one of the
great rivers of the world. Its 820–mile course is dwarfed by the
Nile, the Yangtze, or the Mississippi, and in Europe both the
Volga and the Danube are longer; but none of these rivers can
compare with the Rhine in its diversity of geographical and
historical interest.

Despite such diversity, however, the course of the river falls
into three fairly well defined parts, though each of these has its
own well marked sub-divisions. Rising in Switzerland, on the
southern flank of the St Gotthard massif, the Rhine collects on its
course to Ragaz the glacial waters of the mountains that enclose
the valley of the Bündner Oberland, and flowing through Lake
Constance receives at Coblenz those of a tributary, the Aar, which
carries a greater volume of water than the Rhine itself. In Switzerland, the Rhine flows through the classical land of democratic
freedom, where the Swiss peasants governed themselves under
the maple trees celebrated by Rousseau, in upland valleys un-
touched for centuries by urban civilization. But at Basle the Rhine
leaves Switzerland to enter France and Germany. Here, it has
taken centuries to decide whether freedom or reaction should rule
on the banks of the river, and on its German bank, until very
recently, reaction was triumphant. Finally, the Rhine enters the
wide plain that divides it from the North Sea; at the Dutch

frontier it flows once again into freedom and disperses into the broad and sluggish delta of the Netherlands. The wars that have been fought for possession of the banks of the Rhine have left strategic control of the river to Germany; but it has truly been said that the Rhine can never be a wholly German river because both its mouth and its source belong historically to freedom. Today, however, that contrast has disappeared and the Rhine is free for the whole of its course.

Over two thousand streams contribute to the torrent of waters which meets at Ragaz, on the border between Switzerland and the little principality of Lichtenstein, and any of these might with equal reason be considered the source of the Rhine. They are the product of the Alpine snows and glaciers, ice cold and green, that pour out of the great ring of mountains, from the Todi to the Adula to the Silvretta, which encloses the Swiss canton of the Grisons, or Graubünden, today the paradise of skiers, but once a region of solitude and silence, broken only by the sound of the transport and carriages and marching feet of soldiers and travellers for whom the passes through the Alps provided a way to sunshine and to Italy. The mountains from which the Rhine draws its head waters are all contained within the single canton of the Grisons, once the Roman province of Rhaetia, both the largest and the least populated of the Swiss cantons. Here also rise streams which flow south into Italy and east into the Inn and finally the Danube; the Alpine passes, Oberalp, Lukmanier, Bernardino, Splügen, Septimer, Julier, Albula, all at heights of over 8,000 feet, open the gates through the mountains to the south.

Of all the torrents, however, which spring from the eternal snows, the one which custom has identified as the source of the Rhine is to be found in the south-west corner of the Grisons, on the flank of the Adula massif, the Mons Adulis of Strabo. At its highest point, the Rheinwaldhorn, the range is more than 11,000 feet high; at its foot is the Zoppot glacier, and from this there springs a muddy stream which drops through a ravine which is known to the natives as Hell; not far away, where a few thin traces of vegetation show among the ice and stones, lies Paradise.

From the spring, the stream flows north-east down the pastoral valley of the Rheinwald. From the two little villages of Hinterrhein and Splügen, a road winds upwards to the Bernardino and the Splügen passes; then the stream falls magnificently and precipitately into the gorge of the Rofna, over cataracts and rapids which turn sharply north and continue for three miles until the gorge opens into the valley of Schams. The northern entrance to the valley is closed by another gorge, the Via Mala, three and a half miles long, where the stream becomes a mere white ribbon of water pouring down between limestone precipices 1,600 feet high and barely thirty feet apart, at some points indeed actually overhanging each other. It has been fed, as it emerges from the gorge of La Rofna, by the waters of the Averser Rhein, rising in sources twenty miles to the south and flowing through one of the most beautiful of all Alpine valleys.

The Via Mala ends at Thusis. Here the Hinter Rhein is joined on its left bank, by a small tributary, the Nolla, and below Thusis, on its right bank, by a more important one, the Albula, which is as large as the main river itself. The course of the Albula repeats the same pattern as that of the Hinter Rhein. It reaches Thusis through the Schyn gorge which is as dramatic and headlong as the Via Mala, and above the gorge collects the waters of Alpine valleys similar to those of the Splügen and the Avers; the Davos valley, like the Rheinwald, is high-lying, pastoral and open, and runs down from the pass which leads over to Klosters. Geologists believe that the streams which meet at Klosters from the east and south were once the head waters of the Davos valley and have been captured from it by the same process of erosion which is at work in the Nolla valley.

Above the Schyn gorge, the Albula, as it turns west, receives the waters of the Oberhalbstein Rhein, which runs parallel and west of it. The valley of the Oberhalbstein Rhein once provided, before the railway was constructed, and ever since Roman times, the most direct route across Rhaetia, the Grison of today, running from Tiefencastel up to the Septimer Pass and down into the Val Bregaglia. The Septimer, however, is liable to be closed by avalanches, and the modern road turns aside near the head of the Oberhalbstein valley to cross the Julier Pass, 7,500 feet high, and descend into the valley of the Engadine at Silvaplana. Geological evidence shows that the Oberhalbstein Rhein once flowed at a much higher level than it does today; terraces cut into the sides of the valley show the earlier levels and in places pebbles accumulated on them indicate the sources from which they have been carried.

At Thusis, where the Albula, pouring out of the Schyn gorge, meets the Hinter Rhein, coming from the Via Mala, the river leaves the high snow-peaked Alpine valleys of its sources to enter the lower valleys of the Grison. In the angle formed by the junction of the two rivers, on a high cliff, stands the ruins of the castle of Hohenrhaetien, said to have been built by and named after Rhaetus, the Etruscan leader who was driven out of Italy by the Greeks; its function was to provide a defence against attack from the north. From Thusis, the Hinter Rhein flows through the open Domleschg valley to Reichenau, where it rushes at right angles to meet its sister source of the Rhine, the Vorder Rhein, flowing to meet it from the Oberalp; at their junction the Rhine proper may be said to begin.

The Vorder Rhein is bounded along the whole of its course down to Thusis by the southern face of the great range of mountains which stretches from Oberalp to Ragatz and forms the northern border of the Grison. The peaks of this mountain barrier are from 9,000 to 12,000 feet high, and none of the passes through it are less than 7,000 feet. The torrents that pour down its steep southern slope fall into the long valley of the Bündner Oberland through which the Vorder Rhein flows. The southern drop is so steep that Disentis, at the head of the Bündner Oberland, is only 4,000 feet above sea level and Chur, thirty miles down the valley, only 2,000 feet; northwards, however, the slopes fall gradually into the cantons of Uri, Glarus and St Gallen and to Zurich and the Lake of Lucerne.

The great range of the Tödi is the counterpart of the Rhaetikon range which, with peaks of 9,000 feet and passes of 6,000 feet, strikes north-west from the Silvretta massif and forms the boundary which divides the Grison, and Switzerland, from Austria; at the foot of the range lies the valley of the Prättigau, and Klosters at the head of the valley is less than 4,000 feet above sea level. The two ranges converge at Ragaz; the Alpine basin of the upper waters of the Rhine is completed by the series of snow-crowned peaks and passes which stretches in a great semi-circle from the Silvretta in the east to the Oberalp in the west.

Within this great circle of mountains, the Vorder Rhein, flowing down the Oberalp, collects all the torrents which descend from the range of the Tödi; below Disentis it receives the Medelserrhein, or Middle Rhine, descending from the Lukmanier Pass, which connects it with the Ticino and Lake Maggiore. North of the point at which it joins the Hinter Rhein at Reichenau lies the Kunkels Pass and the valley of the Tamina, which joins the Rhine at Ragaz and cuts off from the main Tödi range the mountain of the Calanda, which rises to 9,000 feet; it is thought that the Hinter Rhein, when flowing at its earlier and higher level, may once have crossed the pass and the Tamina valley, so that Ragaz and not Thusis was the meeting place of the Alpine sources of the Grison.

Further evidence of the great geological changes which have taken place in the Upper Rhine is to be found just above the junction of the Vorder Rhein and the Hinter Rhein at Reichenau. Here both in prehistoric and in historic times there have been vast landslides from the northern walls of the mountains which blocked the course of the river and transformed its upper reaches into a lake. Thus, while the river cut its course through the fallen mass of debris, the road from Ilanz to Reichenau diverges from it and passes further north, high above the river, through pine woods and upland pastures.

Six miles below Reichenau lies Chur, the capital of the Grison. To the south of the town lies the mountain mass encircled by the Prättigau, Davos and Schyn valleys, and itself cut by two deep valleys; on the west, the Lenzerhorn, the dead valley of the earlier Oberhalbstein Rhein, and on the east the winding valley of the Schanfigg, through which the Plessur flows to join the Rhine. On the heights between them stands Arosa.

Chur, with its thirteenth-century cathedral and 15,000 inhabitants, is the ancient Curia Rhaetarum of the Romans and since

Roman times has formed the only urban community and administrative centre of the Grison. In the early Middle Ages, the Bishop of Chur, a Prince of the Holy Roman Empire, together with the Abbot of the great Benedictine abbey of Disentis, exercised temporal power in the Grison, but in the later Middle Ages the peasants revolted against the ecclesiastical magnates and gradually liberated themselves from their rule. The peasant communes grouped themselves into *Gerichte*, literally jurisdictions, or districts, which were in fact independent sovereign states, and were represented by delegates in the three Leagues which were formed to protect their rights; the Ca Dè, or League of the House of God (1368), the Graubund or Grey League (1424), and the Zehngerichtenbund, or League of the Ten Districts (1436). It was a natural consequence of the peasants' conflict with the church, that in the sixteenth century a majority of the population of the Grison adopted the doctrines of the Reformation and became Protestant.

The Ca Dè, with its capital at Chur, included the valleys of the Engadine, the Albula, and the Oberhalbstein Rhein; the Zehngerichtenbund, with its capital at Davos, the Prättigau, the Schanfigg and Davos; the Graubund, whose delegates originally met in the shade of the maple tree at Truns and later had its capital at Ilanz, included the Bündner Oberland, the Valser and Safier valleys, the Rheinwald and Avers. The three Leagues concluded a triple perpetual alliance, which was itself allied with the Swiss Confederation, but it was not until 1799 that Napoleon incorporated the Grison into Switzerland, as part of the Helvetic Republic, and only in 1814 that it became the eighteenth canton of the Swiss Confederation.

The basin of the Upper Rhine, and the immense Alpine ranges which encircle it, have been the determining factors in the history of the Grison, and largely explain how this peasant community should for centuries have been able to maintain its political independence and its democratic form of government; in the Grison indeed, one may find one of the purest forms of democracy in the world. The great range of the Tödi isolated the Grison from the rest of Switzerland, and both historically and geographically gave the sources of the Rhine a different character from the remaining course of the river through Switzerland; in the same way, it divided the peoples of the Swiss Rhine into two distinct communities, those of the Grison and those of the Swiss Confederation. Equally, the Rhaetikon Alps and the range of mountains from the Silvretta to the Oberalp protected the Grison to the east and south.

So far as the peasants of the Grison looked outwards from their mountain fastnesses, it was to Italy and the south, with which the many passes through the Alps gave them communication. To the Romans indeed the Alpine passes gave the Grison, their province of Rhaetia, a particular importance, by providing the most direct route from Germany to Italy, so that in consequence the Grison became very thoroughly Romanized.

The mark of Romanization, together with the effect of the isolation of the remote high-lying valleys of the Upper Rhine basin, is still evident in the linguistic differences that exist between one valley and another and even between different parts of the same valley. The language of nearly a third of the population of the Grison is still a debased dialect of Latin, Romansch in the Bündner Oberland and the Hinter Rhein valley, Ladin in the Engadine.

When at Ragaz the Rhine leaves the Grison, it leaves its birthplace among the Alpine snows, its high-lying valleys which have been the home of individual freedom, its glacial snow-fed torrents, to enter a different world, which is largely an urban and a Germanic one. But it is an essential part of the character of the Rhine, both in the past and today, that its sources are to be found at the foot of the Alpine passes which for centuries have provided a direct link between the north and the south of Europe.

THE SWABIAN RHINE

From Ragaz the Rhine flows thirty miles north to Lake Constance, through a valley enclosed by thickly wooded mountain slopes, which gradually draw apart until at its approach to the lake the plain forms a delta five miles wide. The snows and rains of the Grison make the river here liable to severe flooding. It has been carefully embanked and flows above the level of the plain; the towns on its banks, Feldkirch and Dornbirn on the right, Altstatten on the left, stand away from the river and on the lake itself the ports of Bregenz and Rorschach cling to the firm ground on the edge of the delta.

It is possible that the Rhine at one time did not flow into Lake Constance but followed the Seez valley from Sargans into the lakes of Wallenstadt and Zurich. Now Sargans bars the way into the valley; in the fifteenth century the Swiss purchased its castle because its dominating position controlled the way from the Grison and the Tyrol into the heart of the Confederation. West of Sargans the names of the villages, Prümsch, Siguns, Terzen, Quarten, Quinten derive from the names of the Roman stations, Prima, Secunda, Tertia, Quarta, Quinta, on the road from the Julier pass through Chur to the Roman city of Vindomissa, beyond Zürich.

The angle between the valleys of the present and the earlier course of the Rhine encloses a triangular block of the Alps which includes two Swiss cantons of St Gallen and, an enclave within it, Appenzell; towards the Rhine, and south towards Lake Wallenstadt it presents a steep unbroken face, but to the north-west it slopes gradually down into the Thurgau. From the steep slopes bordering the Rhine two streams, the Thur and the Sitter, flow north-west; the heads of their valleys are commanded by two mountains, to the south the Churfirsten, named for its seven peaks after the seven electors of the medieval empire, rising three thousand feet sheer out of Lake Wallenstadt, and facing it to the north, the beautiful seven thousand foot peak of the Säntis. The Sitter, as it flows through the valley of Appenzell collects the torrents which pour down the northern face of the Säntis.

The canton of St Gallen encloses this entire block of mountains but its enclave of Appenzell includes the peaks of the Säntis, the valley of Appenzell and its tributaries, and a high ridge of Alpine pasture, over a thousand feet above the Rhine valley, which ends abruptly above Lake Constance, near the mouth of the Rhine. These two cantons, with their ravines and lakes, their precipitous peaks and forests, their upland pastures starred in spring by flowers and echoing with the tinkle of cowbells, form one of the most beautiful regions of the Alps. They are also among the most prosperous, the home of peasant industries which in the lower valleys have been further developed by the introduction of electric power; commanding the converging routes of the Rhine and Zürich valleys, they have played a distinctive part in the political development of Switzerland and have also made a notable contribution to the cultural history of Europe.

The great Abbey of St Gallen commemorates the Irish monk who with his companions set out from Ireland for Rome in the seventh century. Taken ill when crossing the Lake of Constance, he landed on its south shores, near Rorschach at the mouth of the Rhine, and one thousand feet above the lake, near the Steinach torrent, built a cell which in time became a place of pilgrimage. There the Abbey was founded, and in the tenth century a wall was built around it for the protection of the monks and their dependants against attack by the Moors from the south and the Magyars from the east. Within the security of its walls, industry, piety and learning flourished at St Gallen; throughout the Dark and Middle Ages its monks pursued the study of both Latin and Greek and preserved and copied the classical texts, and its library today is a marvellous treasury of priceless manuscripts.

In the fourteenth and fifteenth centuries the struggle for political freedom spread to St Gallen from the Forest Cantons and the neighbouring canton of the Grison. The Abbot of St Gallen allied himself to the Hapsburg Duke of Austria against whom the Forest Cantons had revolted. The conflict centred about the Abbot's country villa, the Appenzell or Abbot's cell, in the valley of the Sitter at the foot of the Säntis. Abbot and Duke were defeated at the battle of Stoss Pass, which leads from Alstätten in the Rhine valley to the mountain pastures above St Gallen, and the little republic of Appenzell came into being. It was, however, entirely surrounded by the territory of the Abbot, who continued to control the lower slopes of the mountains, until later St Gallen also joined the Swiss Confederation.

The Reformation split the primitive democracy of Appenzell.

The great Reformer, Zwingli, was born at Wildhaus, within the Abbot's territory; the peasants of the lower slopes of Appenzell to the west, north and north-east adopted the reformed faith and formed their own state of the Ausser Rhoden of Appenzell, while those at the immediate foot of the Säntis, who fed their cattle on its upland pastures, remained faithful to the Catholic religion. For federal purposes, the two Rhodens shared their rights of representation, each sending one delegate to the meetings of the Swiss Federation. Internally, however, the two Rhodens of Appenzell refused to admit the principle of delegation, and each governed itself directly through an assembly of all citizens. The conflict between the Abbot and the citizens of St Gallen continued until the eighteenth century; it was ended by the French Revolution when St Gallen became a part of the Helvetic Republic and later, at the end of the Napoleonic wars, of the Swiss Confederation.

The development of industry has made St Gallen and the Ausser Rhoden of Appenzell one of the most highly populated areas of Switzerland. St Gallen itself, the only large Swiss city which does not stand on a river or a lake, now has a population of over 100,000. The Inner Rhoden, however, still preserves its pastoral simplicity, and only the ancient banners commemorating its past struggle, now in the Office of the Archives in the village of Appenzell, remind a visitor of the significance of its past.

The valley on the eastern slopes of St Gallen and Appenzell through which the Rhine wanders from Sargans to Lake Constance forms the boundary between Switzerland, and the little principality of Lichtenstein, ten miles long, and the Austrian province of the Vorarlberg, which is divided from the Grison in the south by the Rhaetikon Alps and from the Tyrol in the east by the watershed between the Rhine and the Danube. Its people are of the same Swabian stock as the Swiss, while the Tyrolese on the far side of the Arlberg pass are of Bavarian origin; until the Arlberg tunnel penetrated the mountains which divided the Vorarlberg from the Tyrol, the province had a closer affinity with the Swiss than with Austria beyond the Arlberg; but, unlike Switzerland, the Vorarlberg has not been a cradle of political liberty, and for this geography provides some explanation. On the west bank of the Rhine, the steep mountain wall presents an unbroken face to the river and offers no opening to the invader; on the east bank, easy access into the mountains is provided by the valleys of the Ill and the Bregenzer Aach which descend by easy and gradual slopes to the Rhine.

At Rorschach the Rhine enters Lake Constance, the Lacus Brigantinus of the Romans, the Bodensee of the Germans, and the end of the great Roman and medieval route across the Alps to Italy. Forty miles long and ten miles broad, thirteen hundred feet above sea level, at its deepest nine hundred foot deep, it fills completely the gap which lies between the edge of the Alps and the mountains of the Jura which form the boundary between Switzerland and France. It divides the ancient territory of the Swabians into two halves, Swiss on its left bank and German on its right, and because of the obstacles to land travel created by the Alps and the Jura, the easiest communication between them has always been by water so that Lake Constance carries a greater burden of traffic and has a greater commercial importance than any other Alpine lake. In winter ice forms on its shores, once or twice in a century the lake is completely frozen over, but it enjoys a mild and equable climate as so large an expanse of water moderates extremes of temperature and its shores are covered with vineyards and orchards on the slopes of the hills which rise gradually to pastures over a thousand feet high.

Constance is not a Swiss but, completely, an international lake. Each of the states which border, or once bordered on its banks has possessed itself of a portion of them and of a port on its shore. Bregenz, at its eastern end, is Austrian, Lindau Bavarian, Friedrichshafen belonged to Würtemberg and Constance itself to Baden, Romanshorn to the Swiss canton of the Thurgau, and Rorschach, the port of entry for Switzerland's large imports of grain, to St Gallen.

From Rorschach the Rhine flows through the length of the lake and passes under the bridge at Constance into the Unter Sea, or Lower Lake, at a level a few feet lower than the upper lake. Constance itself is a German enclave on the left, or Swiss bank.

During the Middle Ages it was a free city and owed allegiance only to the Emperor. It formed alliances with the Swiss, especially Zürich and Berne, and experienced the same conflicts between citizens and bishops as other Imperial cities. But during the Counter Reformation ecclesiastical rule was restored and Austrians and Spaniards recovered for the Church the city which had been the seat of its greatest Council.

There is evidence to show that the lake was once, at a very much higher level, a tributary of the Danube. It was formed in the Ice Age by the immense glacier which spread outwards from the Rhine valley of the Grison across the plains of Swabia as far as the Jura. Two small tributaries flow into the lake from its German bank; between them and the streams flowing east towards the Danube is a watershed which marks what was once the extreme edge of the glacier. Its effects, together with those of volcanic action, are also to be found in the conical hills, each surmounted by a castle, which rise out of the plain of the Hegau at the north-west end of the lake. They rise two thousand feet above the plain; from one of them, the Hohentviel, one can see the Alps spread before one to the south as far as Mont Blanc.

In the past the Rhine has found different exits from the lake, at one time by its northern arm, the Ueberlinger See, along the present valley of the Stockau and across the Jura, at another from the western end of its southern arm, the Unter See; its present course takes it from the southern arm of the Unter See by a broad navigable channel to Schaffhausen, where once yet another earlier channel led it through the Jura to the valley of the Klettgau. Now the Rhine turns south at Schaffhausen and at Neuhausen, just below it, plunges over a spur of the Jura into the tremendous Falls of the Rhine, nearly a hundred feet high, in a double cataract 370 feet wide carrying 88,000 cubic feet of water a second, swollen to even greater proportions in June and July by the melting snows of the Alps; when sunlight strikes the falls a dazzling iris is formed by the spray thrown off by the tumbling mass of water.

Schaffhausen is Swiss, though on the right bank of the river, and Switzerland has benefited by the electric power generated by the falls, which helps to make the canton of Schaffhausen one of the most prosperous in Switzerland. A few miles below the falls lies the island of Rheinau, the seat of the great Abbey founded in the eighth century, once the home of the Irish monk Findan, and like its sister abbey, founded at the same time on the island of Reichenau further up the river, a memorial to the missionary work of Celtic Christianity in converting the Germans of the Rhine valley. Below Rheinau, at Säckingen, is yet another great monastery founded by the Irish. Säckingen, Rheinau, Reichenau, Constance, St Gallen, Pfäfers, Chur, Disentis are all stations on the great road which made the Rhine valley a route not only for soldiers and merchants, but missionaries, and mark the stages by which the cross was carried into the heart of the Alps.

Between Schaffhausen and Basle the Rhine forms, except for two small areas on its right bank, the boundary between Switzerland and Germany, and receives three important tributaries. From the Alps of St Gallen and Appenzell comes the Thur, liable to severe flooding from the Alpine snow; at Swiss Coblenz, 'the meeting of the waters', it receives both the Wutach, on its right bank, bringing down the waters of the Black Forest and, most important of all, from the south a river even greater than itself at that point, the Aar, which carries into the Rhine two thirds of the drainage of Switzerland.

At Coblenz the Rhine has penetrated through the Jura, which it entered at Eglisau, and has collected all the waters of its Alpine sources; its waters are green and transparent as it pours through its valley between the Jura and the Black Forest, over the salmon falls of Laufenburg and the rapids at Rheinfelden, and making a great curve from the west to the north, passes under the bridge at Basle and leaves Switzerland for Germany and France.

THE AAR

Though the Rhine finds its furthest sources in the Alps of the Grison, and the glaciers of the Oberalp and the St Gottard, it is not in fact from them that it derives the great bulk of its waters. This it receives at its junction at Coblenz with the Aar; above

Coblenz the Rhine carries a smaller volume of water than is brought into it by its tributary. The waters of the Aar come from the streams which drain the northern slope of the continuous mountain wall which extends for 120 miles from Chur on the Rhine to Martigny on the Rhône. This great range forms the precipitous northern face of the valley at its foot, which to the north-east is drained by the Rhine and to the south-west by the Rhône. At either end its peaks rise to over 7,000 feet, the Finsteraarhorn in its centre is over 14,000 feet, and none of its passes are lower than 7,000 feet, except where the river Reuss, a tributary of the Aar, rising south of the range, drives straight through it by a precipitous gorge which is cut to a depth of only 4,000 feet above sea level.

The Reuss rises between the sources of the Rhône and the Vorder Rhein, at the head of the Urseren valley by which the road from Martigny up the Valais to the Rhône glacier and the Furka Pass, over 8,000 feet high, continues to Andermatt and over the Oberalp pass to Disentis and Chur. Through the Urseren valley the road and the river follow the same course; at Andermatt, however, the Reuss changes course sharply from east to north and by a granite-walled gorge in which it falls a thousand feet cuts its way into the valley of Uri.

Up to the thirteenth century the Schollenen gorge was impassable. There was no road from Uri into the Urseren valley and its Romansch speaking people, though under the nominal rule of the Abbot of Disentis, were virtually independent. In the twelfth century the Devil's Bridge was thrown over the Reuss to serve a mule path through the gorge; it survived until the end of the nineteenth century when it was destroyed by flood. In the eighteenth century a tunnel two hundred feet long, the Urnerloch, was pierced into the wall of the gorge to carry the high road out of Urseren and beyond it a single one hundred foot span bridge was built over what are now the ruins of the Devil's Bridge.

From the Schollenen gorge the Reuss flows north through the valley of the Uri, and at Flüelen enters the Urner See or Lake of Uri, the southern arm of the Lake of Lucerne, the heart and centre of the original Switzerland. This position it acquired as the natural centre of communications between the four forest cantons bordering its shore, of which Uri was almost inaccessible by land and the three others hardly less so. When the Hapsburgs became lords of Lucerne, it was natural that the four cantons should fear the loss of the independence which was the product of their isolation, and league themselves to defend it.

Thirty miles north of Lucerne, where the Reuss meets with the Limmat and the Aar, and just south of the confluence of Aar and Rhine at Coblenz, on a wooded hill, lies the Hawk's Castle, or Habichtsburg, the cradle of the Imperial house of Austria.

For nearly a thousand years, the family historyof the Hapsburgs was a part of the history of Europe. Albert of Hapsburg, who died in 1199, became Count of Zürich and Landgrave of Upper Alsace. His son Rudolf acquired Laufenberg and the protectorate over the Swiss forest cantons of Schwyz, Uri, Unterwalden and Lucerne. In 1273, Rudolf 1 was elected King of Germany; to the duchies of Austria and Styria which he bestowed on his sons, their successors added the Tyrol, Vorarlberg, Carinthia, Carniola and Gorizia. After 1282, the Hapsburgs were dukes and archdukes of Austria; after 1526, kings of Hungary and Bohemia; from 1438–1806, Holy Roman Emperors; from 1516–1700, kings of Spain; after 1804, emperors of Austria. For a brief moment a Hapsburg, Maximilian 1, brother of the Emperor Francis Joseph, even became Emperor of Mexico, before being executed by a firing squad. The position of the castle of Hapsburg has a magnificence, and commands an outlook, which seem to foreshadow the imperial destiny of the Hapsburgs; close by stretches, as far as the eye can see, the whole of the south-eastern face of the Jura; below lies the plain of Switzerland and beyond it the snow peaks of the Alps. At the foot of the hill, lies the site of the Roman city of Vindonissa, and near by, on the Limmat, the little town of Baden, which was for centuries the seat of the Swiss Parliament, and a crossing of the Aar from which roads lead west over the Jura to Säckingen and Basle, on the Rhine, north to Coblenz, east up the Limmat to Zürich, south-east up the Reuss to Zürich, south-west up the Aar to Neuchâtel. Each of the three rivers which meet at Hapsburg has its own way over the Alps to the south; up the Limmat to Lakes Zürich and Wallenstadt, Sargans and the Grison and the passes to Lake Como; up the Reuss to Lucerne, the Schollenen gorge, Urseren, the St Gottard and Lake Maggiore and by the Lake of Geneva to the St Bernard.

The rivers find their sources in three great icefields of the Bernese Oberland which stretches for sixty miles from the Diablerets to the Grimsel Pass and the Rhône glacier. On the west it rises to the peaks of Diablerets, Wildhorn, Wildstrube, Balmhorn, all between 10,000 and 12,000 feet, with passes of from 7,000 to 8,000 feet; on the east the valley of the Rhône encloses the largest icefield in the Alps, twenty-five miles long by five miles broad, rising to the Finsteraarhorn. East of the icefield is the Grimsel Pass leading to the Hasli valley and the head waters of the Aar. Beyond the Hasli valley the icefield is renewed, with the Rhône glacier on its south-western slope, and immediately east of it the gorge of the Reuss; beyond again is the icefield of the Tödi, from which springs the Linth or, as it is known after leaving Lake Zürich, the Limmat. Thus the ice of the front range of the Alps forms three great fields, divided by the Aar valley and the Reuss gorge, from which the Aar, the Reuss and the Limmat flow down to the Rhine.

The streams from the Oberaar and Unteraar glaciers, descending from the Finsteraarhorn into the Hansli valley, unite at the foot of the Grimsel Pass and turning north pour through a magnificent gorge over the falls of Handeck, 130 feet high; the stream passes through pine forests and an open valley until it cuts its way through another, hardly less magnificent gorge into a lower level of the valley at Meiringen, then turns west and enters the Lake of Brienz and the Lake of Thun, divided by Interlaken. From the Jungfrau to the south, the Lütschine and the Lauter-brunnen valleys descend to Interlaken, the Lütschine carrying with it the waters which the Grindelwald valley, to the east, has brought down from the Obergrindelwald and Utergrindelwald glaciers; Lake Thun collects the waters of the Kanderthal and Simmerwald valleys. Thus when it leaves Interlaken and Lake Thun the Aar has been fed by all the streams of the mountains and passes from the Wildhorn to the Grimsel and forms the most important head stream of all the sources of the Rhine.

Below Thun, the Aar, still at a height of 1,500 feet, cuts its way through the foothills of the Alps into the plain of Berne, and making a loop round the town receives from the west the Saane descending from the Bernese Oberland and draining all the valleys west of the Simmerwald. Where the river leaves the mountains, about twenty miles up stream from Berne, stands Freiburg, Catholic and still half French speaking, which was once an outpost in the Rhine basin of the medieval kingdom of Burgundy. Within ten miles of it is the little town of Avenches, the Roman Aventicum, stationed on the road from Lake Geneva to Vindonissa and Lake Constance.

To the west of the junction of the Aar and the Saane lies Lake Neuchâtel, the largest of all the wholly Swiss lakes, with Lakes Morat and Bienne. Unlike the other lakes of the Rhine basin, they lie parallel with the line of the Alps and not across it, they have low shores and are not fed by any important streams, for those of the Jura flow west into the Rhône and the Saane carries those of the Freiburg Alps directly into the Aar. In the history of Switzerland the lakes played an important part as a defensive barrier to the north-west; on their shores, in the fifteenth century, at the decisive battles of Morat and Grandson the Swiss defeated the invasion launched by the Duke of Burgundy from across the Jura.

In Lake Bienne is the Isle-St-Pierre, or St-Peter-Insel, where Rousseau once found refuge from delusions of persecution. Below its junction with the Saane, the Aar has been diverted into the lake by canal from its original course, in order to moderate the effect of flood water pouring down from its glacier fed sources in the Alps. Nature has designed the Lakes of Constance, Zürich and Lucerne to perform a similar function for the Rhine, the Limmat and the Reuss; the only Swiss tributaries of the Rhine which are not so protected against flood are the two Emmen streams flowing down between Lucerne and Thun, the Sihl from the hills between Lucerne and Zürich, and the Thun from the Säntis area of St Gallen and Appenzell, but none of these is glacier fed.

The basin of the Aar contains within it all the cantons out of which modern Switzerland developed. In the Middle Ages, the main north-south road through Switzerland ran over the Jura from the Rhine at Basle, past Hapsburg to Zürich and the Lake of Zürich, and on to Sargans, Chur, the Lenzeheath, the passes of the Rhaetikon Alps, Lake Como and Milan. An east-west cross route ran from Schaffhausen on the Rhine to the shores of Lake Constance, Zürich, Berne, Freiburg, Lausanne and Lake Geneva. Lucerne, the heart of the original compact between the four Forest Cantons of Uri, Schwyz, Unterwalden and Lucerne lay aside from both routes and only became important as a result of the compact itself. Switzerland itself takes its name from the canton of Schwyz, the most exposed of all the four cantons to attack by the Counts of Hapsburg, frequently in alliance with Zürich. The fifth and sixth members of the Federation were Zug, and Glarus in the valley of the Linth and the seventh and eighth Zürich and Berne; the eight cantons completed medieval Switzerland and all lay within the basin of the Aar and the Rhine.

The original cantons expanded to the east by purchasing the strategically important castle of Sargans, and from the valley of Uri, or Altdorf, the home of William Tell, pushed east over the Klausen pass, west over the Suranen Pass, and south up the valley of the Reuss into the Urseren valley and beyond it into the Ticino. Urseren and the Ticino, Romansch and Italian speaking, fell to German speaking Uri by right of conquest, and in turn the opening of the road south through the Reuss valley diverted the main European route from north to south from Sargans and Chur to Lucerne and the St Gottard, through the heart of the Forest Cantons. In its origins, free Switzerland may properly be described as a German speaking Rhenish Confederation.

3 The Upper German Rhine

BASLE TO BINGEN

At Basle the Rhine bends from its westerly course to the north, and for about 180 miles flows through the wide depression known as the Rhine Rift valley, or *Graben*. For the first 120 miles of its course through the valley, past Mulhouse, Colmar, Freiburg-im-Breisgau and Strasbourg, the river forms the boundary between France and Germany; on its left bank lie the historic lands of Alsace which were seized by the Germans from France in 1870, restored in 1918, re-annexed to Germany in 1940 and restored once more to France in 1945. At its northern end, the Rift valley is blocked by the line of the Taunus mountains, which once again force the river on a westerly course to Bingen, where it enters the eighty-mile long gorge of the Middle Rhine between Bingen and Bonn. The river, indeed, at the northern end of the valley repeats the same pattern in relation to the mountains which surround it as at its entry at the southern end of the Rift valley at Basle.

The Rift valley of the Rhine, especially on its first seventy miles between Basle and Strasbourg, is both one of the most interesting and one of the most beautiful natural features of Europe. The steep slopes of the Vosges on the west bank and of the Black Forest on the east rise to a height of nearly 5,000 feet; the flat fertile bottom of the valley between them is nearly twenty miles broad and covered by orchards and cultivated fields which yield crops of maize, hops and tobacco. The river, with its tributary, the Ill, flowing parallel to it on the west, on its course through the valley falls four hundred feet between Basle and Strasbourg. As they rise from the valley, the steep slopes of the mountains on either hand are terraced by vineyards, which give way to a dark green ribbon of pine forests and finally to open upland pastures.

On either bank, both the Vosges and the Black Forest show their steepest slopes to the river, mountain edges that rise sharply out of the valley. They once formed part of a great mountain range that ran across this area in a direction roughly parallel with the Alps. In prehistoric times it sank beneath the sea and was covered by soft deposits from the shores which surrounded it; then under tremendous pressure was hurled to the surface again and torn apart, so that great blocks of it were raised as vast plateaux whose surface was denuded of its soft deposits by the weather and the granite of the ancient mountain range stood out from the surrounding plain of limestone and clay. The Vosges and the Black Forest together formed one of these great plateaux; the Rhine valley was formed by a rift or fault running through it from south-south-west to north-north-east. The steep fronts of the mountains represented the edges of the fault; the valley bed of the Rhine was formed by the heights of the plateau which had collapsed between them. Where the Rhine enters the rift valley, its course is almost blocked by the northern end of the Jura, and the river has cut a deep passage between them and the Black Forest. West of Basle, however, the edge of the Jura and the foot of the Vosges are separated by nearly twenty miles. This open, riverless plain is the famous Gate of Burgundy, the *trouée de Belfort*, or Belfort Gap, one of the decisive strategical features of Europe, through which once the ancient Burgundians, the people of the *Nibelungenlied*, found their way from their capital at Worms on the Rhine to their permanent land of settlement, and where for centuries armies have marched and countermarched. Belfort, which commands the gap has been repeatedly besieged, five times in the seventeenth century and again in 1814 and 1815; invested by the Germans during the Franco-Prussian War on 3 November, 1870, it held out heroically and was still in French hands after the conclusion of the armistice which ended the war in February 1871.

Where the Rhine flows between them north of Basle, the Vosges and the Black Forest are at their highest; from a peak like the Blauen in the Black Forest one can look far away over the river to the misty summits of the Vosges in the west and south over the foothills of the Jura to the snows of the Alps. Or again at Alt-Breisach, halfway between Basle and Strasbourg, facing across the river the fortress of Neu-Breisach constructed by Vauban, where the Rhine flows swiftly and powerfully at the foot of a rock on which stood an earlier fortress, one may climb the group of isolated, vineyard covered, volcanic hills known as the Kaiserstuhl, where the Holy Roman Emperors once dispensed justice to their subjects. They rise to 1,000 feet above the plain and command a marvellous panoramic view of the rift valley, to the west the Vosges, to the east the Black Forest, to the south the Jura, between them the Belfort Gap opening to a limitless horizon, and sometimes in the distance to the north the beautiful delicate Gothic spires of the cathedral at Strasbourg.

Strasbourg itself lies three miles west of the river. Indeed it is one of the charms of the Rhine on this stretch of its course north of Basle that except for Breisach there are no towns of any size on its banks. For the river itself, until it was brought under control, frequently altered its course through the shifting sands and gravels of the valley, and the low water meadows on either bank offered poor ground for cultivation. Settlement kept away from the river and clung to the foot of the mountains, where towns grew up, Mulhouse, Colmar and Schlettstadt on the left bank, Freiburg, Lahn and Offenburg on the right, which formed a strip of dense and continuous population. Thus it can properly be said that the Rhine here genuinely formed a natural frontier which held apart the people of Alsace and those of the Black Forest.

The Romans approached this stretch of the Rhine through the Gate of Burgundy, north of which lay their province of First Germany, occupying the land between the Vosges and the Rhine. West of Basle they founded the town of Augusta; the next station on their soldiers' road was Strasbourg itself, where the river Zorn joins the Rhine by a gorge cut through the Vosges into the rift valley. Through the gorge came the Roman road from Metz, past the station of *Tres Tabernae*, which is the modern Zabern. Thus Basle itself was not of Roman origin. It is first heard of in the fourth century. Its commercial importance, and its modern development as a great centre of communications was based on its position at the head of the boat navigation of the Rhine and on the medieval roads from west to east up the Rhine valley to the Lake of Constance. In the Middle Ages it became an imperial free city and in the sixteenth century allied itself to the Swiss Confederation.

The place of the Romans in the Upper rift valley was taken by the Allemanni, or Swabians, who occupied the basin of the Aar, the banks of Lake Constance and the upper reaches of the Danube, the basin of the Neckar and the rift valley of the Rhine as far as Baden-Baden; their frontier to the west corresponded roughly to the modern language frontier between French and German which runs along the watershed of the Vosges. Thus the plain of modern Alsace belonged to the Allemanni, who included under their rule the Nordgau of Strasbourg, the Sundgau of Mulhouse, and the Breisgau, across the Rhine, in the angle formed by the northward bend of the river at Basle.

In the Breisgau, where the mountains of the Black Forest make an easterly curve from the river, and the waters of the Dreisam come down to join the Rhine, on the heights above the Dreisam valley, there stand the ruins of the castle of the ancient family of Zähringen, lords of the Breisgau, in the eleventh and twelfth centuries. The founders both of Berne and of Freiburg-im-Breisach, they also founded at the foot of their castle the city of Freiburg-im-Bresigau which today, with its lovely sandstone cathedral and its streets that are washed and freshened by the waters of the Dreisam which run in rivulets through their gutters, is perhaps the most agreeable of all German university towns. The Zähringen ruled both the Breisgau and the Sundgau across the river; when the family became extinct in 1264, they were replaced in the Breisgau by the Hapsburgs, who were not ejected from it until the French Revolution.

Beyond Freiburg, the curve of the Black Forest returns again towards the Rhine, in a semi-circle which is almost completed by the detached group of the Kaiserstuhl; the steep face which the mountains present to the river in the plain beneath them forms a continuous wall of granite as far as the mouth of the Kinzig valley, opposite Strasbourg.

Here the Rhine receives not only, on its right bank, the Kinzig, but on its left bank the Zorn, from the Gate of Zabern, and the Reusch; the Kinzig and the Reusch are indeed the most important of the tributaries which it receives from the Black Forest and the Vosges, and their valleys, together with that of the Zorn, make Strasbourg, the capital of Alsace, the natural centre of this section of the Rhine rift valley. Up the Kinzig valley runs the Black Forest railway past Offenburg to the waterfall at Tribourg and over the mountains and through the upper valley of the Danube to Schaffhausen and Lake Constance; a light railway also crosses the Black Forest from Freiburg and through the gorge of the Höhlenthal to the upper Danube. The ascent of both the Kinzig and the Höhlen valleys, however, is steep and makes gradients difficult; thus the great trans-European line of the Orient Express swerves north away from Strasbourg at Zabern and leaves the Rhine valley behind Karlsruhe by the easier route over the foot-hills of the Black Forest.

The Breisgau, one of the most beautiful regions of Germany, belongs today to the state of Württemberg-Baden, but until 1918 formed part of the Grand Duchy of Baden, which from the fall of Napoleon ruled the whole of the right bank of the Rhine from Lake Constance to Heidelberg, except for Swiss outposts at Schaffhausen and opposite Basle. The Grand Dukes of Baden were lineal descendants of the house of Zähringen; the ruins of their ancient tower of Hohenbaden stands high on the crest of the mountains above the little valley of the Oos. As their style and pretensions increased, the counts and margraves of Baden descended from their mountain fastness to build first a renaissance palace at Neubaden, near the thermal springs at Baden-Baden which the Romans had patronized, and which in the eighteenth century became a centre of fashion for the European nobility and intelligentsia; and later to create toy replicas of Versailles at Rastatt and Karlsruhe, of which the second became the capital of the Grand Duchy.

Opposite Karlsruhe two tributaries of the Rhine, the Lauter and the Quelch descend from the hills bordering the left bank of the river. They form roughly the language frontier which divided the dialects of the Allemanni and the Franks, and at different times each has been the northern boundary of Alsace. From the time of Louis xiv, Landau on the Quelch was garrisoned by the French, but from the end of the Napoleonic wars the Lauter became the French frontier. In the war of 1870, the left wing of the German army formed up behind the Lauter, advanced to besiege and capture Strasbourg, but failed to take Belfort, so that the southern part of the ancient Sundgau remained French and the Franco-German frontier between 1870 and 1918 roughly corresponded to the watershed that divides the Rhine and the Rhône. But though Alsace was conquered, and was to be conquered again, the French had left a permanent mark on the geography of the region in the canals which joined the Rhine to the Rhône through the Belfort Gap and the Marne to the Rhine through the Gate of Zabern.

NECKAR AND MAIN

The Kinzig valley opposite to Strasbourg makes a break in the steep cliff edge which the mountains of the Black Forest present to the Rhine. As the height of the mountains declines from the Kinzig valley to beyond Baden-Baden, the sandstone of their gentler eastern slopes advances west and takes the place of the granite face exposed to the river. Further north, to just south of Heidelberg, where the mountains fall away from the river, sandstone gives way to a peculiarly rich and fertile belt of limestone. Then the land rises sharply again to the mountains of the Odenwald, whose granite face stretches north to Darmstadt and then turns away east towards Aschaffenburg.

Out of the Odenwald, through steep gorges cut through the sandstone of its eastern slopes and the granite of its western and northern ones, come two of the Rhine's most important tributaries, the Neckar and the Main, which enter the Rhine valley at Heidelberg and Aschaffenburg. Both belong essentially to the great water network of the Rhine basin and each has made its own particular contribution, geographical and historical, to the life of the area which is bound together by the river. Both rise to the east of the mountain edge which overlooks the Rhine valley and drain a large area in which are also to be found the head waters of the Danube.

The Neckar, 230 miles long, rises near Schwenningen, close to the sources of the Danube, flows north and north-east along the foot of the Swabian Jura, past Rothweil, Rothenburg and Tübingen, changes its course northwards away from the mountains, and through Cannstadt, near Stuttgart, follows a broad deep vineyard-laden valley, winding between hills that above the vineyards are crowned by castles, past Heilbronn and Wimpfen to Eberbach. There the river turns west on a sinuous and tortuous course that takes it between wooded heights past the foot of the Kaiserstuhl and under the walls of Heidelberg to join the Rhine at Mannheim.

The beauty of the Neckar valley makes it appropriate that it should have given birth to two of Germany's greatest poets, Schiller and Hölderlin. Schiller was born in 1759 at the little town of Marbach, near Stuttgart, where the poet is commemorated by the Schiller National Museum. He was educated, one might almost say forcibly, in the military schools maintained by Duke Karl Eugen of Württemberg at Ludwigsberg and Stuttgart. He was hardly more than a schoolboy when he wrote his first play *Die Raüber*, which caused as great a sensation in Germany as Goethe's *Gotz von Berlichingen*, written eight years earlier.

Goethe and Schiller indeed might have been regarded as the two poles of the genius of the Rhineland, the one conservative, Olympian and classical, the second radical, romantic and dominated by the wild medley of ideas of the German *Sturm und Drang*. Yet, opposed as they were, friendship with Goethe became the most importance influence in Schiller's life; he tried to define the difference between them in his famous essay *On Sentimental and Naive Poetry*, which has had a permanent influence on all subsequent theories of aesthetics. In 1799 he took up permanent residence at Weimar, in order to live close to his friend, and in an outburst of creative energy wrote the great series of plays, *Wallenstein, Maria Stuart, Die Jüngfrau von Orleans, Die Braut von Messina* and *Wilhelm Tell*, which preceded his death in 1805.

Goethe was one of those great men on whom fortune smiles. Schiller was not, and his life was darkened by ill health, poverty, and an intensely susceptible and irritable temperament. Even so, it did not equal Hölderlin's in tragedy. He was born not far from Schiller's birthplace at Lauffen-am-Neckar in 1770 and died seventy-three years later at Tübingen, in a little room belonging to the carpenter Zimmerman overlooking the Neckar; there he spent the last thirty-six years of his life in a condition of hopeless and incurable insanity.

Hölderlin's poetry has bathed the landscape of the Rhine and its tributaries, the Neckar and the Main, in the golden light of classical Greece, and made its hills and streams the dwelling place of gods and heroes. More even than Goethe he gave expression to the German nostalgia for the sunny lands of the Mediterranean, and the classical art and literature to which they gave birth; but what is rarer, and indeed unique, is that he actually brought their spirit to life again on the banks of the Neckar and the Main, so that one seems to see the footprints of the sun god as he passes across them.

The Main, 325 miles long, is the most important tributary which the Rhine receives on its right bank. It has two sources, the Weisser Main, rising in the Fichtel Gebirge, a bare, bleak mountain group in Bavaria, and the Rote Main, rising on the eastern slopes of the Franconian Jura. The Weisser Main joins its sister river at Kulmbach, circles the northern end of the Franconian Jura at Bamberg, where it receives its chief tributary the Regnitz, and becomes navigable for barges and small craft. From Bamberg, it flows through a deep vineclad valley to Würzburg and turns north, between the forest covered ranges of the Odenwald and the Spessart, to Gemünden, and makes a sharp turn south to Wertheim, where it receives one of the most beautiful of German rivers, the Tauber. There it turns west and north again to Aschaffenburg and passes Frankfurt to join the Rhine.

The north-eastern edge of the Neckar basin is bounded by the Thüringer Wald, which strikes north-west from the Fichtel Gebirge until it approaches the plateau which the Rhine pierces at Bingen. Between them lies the gap by which the Werra finds its way to the north; south of the gap lie two volcanic mountain groups, the Vogels Berg and the Rhön, of which the Rhön extends south into the Spessart, in the southern loop of the Main between Gemünden and Aschaffenburg and continues, across the gorge of the Main, into the sandstone eastern slopes of the Odenwald.

The basins of the Neckar and the Main are wholly enclosed by a great circle of mountain ranges which extends from the Black Forest in the south along the Jura to the Fichtel Gebirge in the east, and north-west along the Thüringer Wald to the Taunus. From this mountain ring the Danube and its tributaries, the Altmühl and the Wornitz, break out through the Jura to the south, the Main through the Spessart to the north-west and the Neckar through the southern slopes of the Odenwald. This great land-locked area, which contains some of the most beautiful regions of Germany, a land of mountains and deep, sheltered, grape-laden valleys, embraces what used to be Franconia and Swabia and now belongs to the states of Württemberg-Baden and Bavaria, so that the whole of the Main and Neckar basins lie within the boundaries of the German Federal Republic.

Both Neckar and Main share in the beauty and fertility of the low-lying belt of land which, within the arms of the mountains, stretches from the Spessart to the Jura. But historically their destinies have been different. The Neckar is the river of Swabia, and the castle ruins which stand on the hills that overlook its banks commemorate petty principalities which in the Middle Ages made Swabia the most violently divided and fragmented of all the German states; though among them were also dynasties like the Hohenstaufen and the Hohenzollern which rose to imperial greatness. It was only at the end of the Middle Ages that the Counts of Württemberg established their pre-eminence, symbolized by their residence at Stuttgart, in a little valley in the sandstone hills which open out to the Neckar at Cannstadt; it was not until Napoleon had extinguished the other petty states of Swabia that Württemberg became a kingdom, extending south beyond the Jura and across the Danube to the Lake of Constance at Friedrichshafen. All that remained of those who had once fought so fiercely was the little state of Hohenzollern-Sigmaringen, which in the middle of the last century became a detached province of Prussia.

In the Franconian basin of the Main, however, the strongest temporal power was that of the Church, which advanced from the great missionary centre at Mainz along the river, establishing itself at Aschaffenburg, Würzburg and Bamberg, so that the valley of the Main became famous, or notorious, as the Priests' Alley. Aschaffenburg became the administrative centre of the wide temporal jurisdiction of the Archbishops of Mainz; the Bishops of Würzburg and Bamberg were almost equally powerful. Secular dynasties only established themselves on the Main at Bayreuth, at the head of the valley, and at Ansbach; Nuremberg, Schweinfurt and Rothenburg achieved independence and prosperity as free imperial cities. The power of the Church in Franconia endured until the Napoleonic wars and in the European settlement that followed nearly the whole of the Main basin was transformed to Bavaria.

There was one further important historical difference between the basins of the Neckar and the Main, for Swabia was to some extent Romanized while Franconia was not. When the Roman frontier lay east of the Rhine, one section of it was formed by the Main south of Aschaffenburg, and was continued by a line of entrenchments running directly south to Lorch and the province of Rhaetia. From Lorch the frontier turned east along the foot of the Jura and then over the mountains to the Danube; thus Swabia on the Neckar and Bavaria on the Danube lay within the Roman frontier, while Franconia on the Main lay beyond it.

Ringed by their wall of mountains in the heart of Europe, the Neckar and Main basins provided important links in the lines of communication which meet on the Rhine. One runs up the Main valley from Aschaffenburg to Bamberg, where one road forks up the upper Rhine valley into Saxony and a second along the Regnitz valley to Nuremberg. There one route proceeds south-east via Ratisbon to the Danube, and another south-west to the Danube at Donaueschingen and via Augsburg over the Brenner to Italy.

Both Nuremberg and Bamberg profited from their position as centres of these important lines of communication. The Neckar has no towns of similar historical significance, for Stuttgart, though now a great industrial city, was the artificial creation of a court and of relatively recent origin. The Neckar, however, has its part in the main east route across Europe. The roads from Vienna and Italy through Ulm on the Danube continue over the Jura into the Neckar valley at Esslingen, along the river to Cannstadt and over to Pforzheim, and into the Rhine valley at Karlsruhe; across the Rhine, the road continues through the gate of Zabern to Lorraine and Paris.

Where the Neckar joins the Rhine below Heidelberg, the rift valley of the upper Rhine draws to an end, and in leaving the valley the river reproduces the pattern of its entry into it at Basle. The line of the Taunus blocks the northern end of the valley just as the Jura block its southern end; and just as the Jura leave the broad plain of the Belfort Gap between themselves and the Vosges, so the Taunus leave between themselves and the Odenwald the gap by which the Main passes by Frankfurt to join the Rhine at Mainz.

The Taunus, at the northern end of the valley, reach only half the height of the Vosges and Black Forest at its southern end; at their highest point, however, the Feldberg, near Bad Homberg, they rise to nearly 2,800 feet and from the summit command a magnificent outlook over the river. Below are the forested slopes of the mountains, falling to the terraced vineyards of the Rheingau between Weisbaden and Rüdesheim, the waters of the Rhine and the Main and the dense industrial concentration surrounding Frankfurt. To the south-west are the summits of the Odenwald and beyond them the open plain of the Rhine valley. From the south come the two roads running parallel at the foot of the mountains on either side of the valley, ending at Mainz and Frankfurt; on the right bank is the autobahn from Basle to Frankfurt, running past Freiburg, Karlsruhe, Heidelberg, Mannheim and Darmstadt. From the north come the two roads which fork at Kassel, where the Weser flows north to the sea, and follow the valleys of the Main tributaries, the Kinzig and the

Nidda. Looking down at the industrial haze over Frankfurt, one is looking at a city which is at the centre of a road and river network which stretches to Italy, the Mediterranean, Paris, the Danube and the North Sea, and of this network the Rhine itself is the main artery.

Nature and geography would seem to have designed the northern end of the Rhine rift valley as the site of one of the great capitals of Europe. Both Frankfurt on the Main and Mainz on the Rhine would, by their position, have been adapted to play such a part, and each in the past has had its moments of greatness; but history, assisted in recent times by Dr Adenauer, has decided against them.

In the case of Mainz, it should be remembered that the Rhine itself has suffered geological changes which until modern times have created obstacles to navigation on the river and to through communication to the sea. Once the river flowed high above its present level over the site of Mainz, but geological changes lowered its bed so that at one time at Mainz it was five hundred feet below sea level while at Bingen it was five hundred feet above it. Such changes were so slow that the Rhine preserved its course, cutting a way for itself through the new foundations. But until comparatively recent times the obstacles raised at the entry of the gorge at Bingen remained a serious hindrance to navigation.

Mainz was, however, the most important of the three cities, Mainz, Worms and Speyer, which the Romans founded in the Rhine rift valley. Both on its right and its left bank, the Rhine at Mainz provide solid ground which was suitable for building and for the construction of approach roads, so that it formed a natural bridging site. The foundations of the Roman bridge and for the fort built for its protection on the left bank still remain; when the frontier was advanced beyond the river by Domitian, the suburb of Castel was built as a bridgehead on the right bank. Mainz lay within the protection of the *Pfalgraben*, or entrenchments, which the Romans built northwards from the Main as it emerges from the Spessart; they enclosed the fertile valley of the Wetterau and after turning towards the Rhine along the summits of the Taunus, bent north again to protect the right bank of the Rhine as far as Coblenz. Within the line of the frontier, four miles from Mainz on the right bank of the river, lies Wiesbaden, which the Romans patronized as a suburban resort on account of its thermal springs.

With the decline of Rome, Mainz lost its pre-eminence among the Rhine cities to Worms, which for a time flourished, and earned itself immortality in epic and romance, as the capital of the Burgundians on their long trek down the Rhine valley and through the Belfort Gap into the basin of the Rhône. It was there that Siegfried betrayed Kriemhild; there that Hagen slew Siegfried; there that Hagen cast the treasure of the Nibelungen into the Rhine.

Mainz regained its importance in the Middle Ages as the centre of the great missionary effort conducted by its Archbishops beyond the Rhine; the arms of the city, a pair of wheels, are those of the English St Boniface, a wheelwright's son and first Archbishop of Mainz. As in other cities of the Rhine, however, the citizens of Mainz revolted against the temporal power of their Archbishops; in 1254, Mainz, in alliance with Worms, formed a great league of Rhineland cities which stretched from Basle in the south to Cologne in the north. Under the protection of the League, commerce prospered on the Rhine for the next two centuries and Mainz, because of its wealth, earned the name of the Golden City.

But in 1462, the Archbishop of Mainz re-established the power of the Church, and Mainz lost its commercial pre-eminence to the imperial free city of Frankfurt. It retained the distinction of being the seat of the Primate Archbishop of Germany, one of the three ecclesiastical electors of the Empire, and the magnificence of its great Romanesque and Gothic cathedral. As elsewhere, it remained for Napoleon to put an end to ecclesiastical rule at Mainz. During the nineteenth century, Prussia and Austria jointly garrisoned the city on behalf of the German Confederation, but in 1870 its ramparts were destroyed and the city entered on a renewed period of commercial prosperity.

Frankfurt on the Main, like Mainz on the Rhine, owes its historic importance to its position as a centre of communications, and especially to the road which, over the bridge at Frankfurt, joins Marburg and Giessen in the north to Darmstadt and thence to Heidelberg in the south. Like Mainz also, its site had the advantage of firm ground on both banks of the river. Unlike Mainz, however, it is not of Roman origin; its history begins as the capital of Charlemagne's empire, where the Holy Emperors were chosen until the extinction of the Empire in 1806. But the true source of its development in the Middle Ages was the privileges it enjoyed as a free city, and the protection and patronage extended by the Emperor to its great Easter and Autumn fairs, which played the same part in medieval commercial life in the west as the great Russian fair at Nijni-Novgorod in the east.

As a free city, Frankfurt prospered for centuries, and even after the Napoleonic wars emerged, with the three Hanseatic towns of North Germany, as a sovereign city state. During the revolution of 1848, it became the seat of the all-German parliament, and for a moment it seemed that Frankfurt might become the first capital of a free, democratic and united Germany. Such hopes were defeated by the young Bismarck, and after the Austro-Prussian war of 1866, in which the city had allied itself with Austria, Frankfurt suffered the humiliation of annexation to Prussia. After the Second World War, and the defeat of a Germany which had been made in the image of Prussia, it seemed as if once again Frankfurt might become, as it was well fitted to be, the capital of a free and democratic Germany orientated towards the west. Once again, history decided otherwise.

Above Frankfurt, on the Main, lies Aschaffenburg, the second great ecclesiastical centre in the Priests' Alley which extended up the Main to Würzburg and Bamberg. Between Frankfurt and Aschaffenburg, on opposite sides of the Main, lie the two industrial towns of Offenburg and Hainau, which owe their growth to settlement, in the one case, by Protestant Dutchmen and in the other by Huguenot Frenchmen. Like the small industrial towns and villages along the Rhine, in the Swiss cantons, the Black Forest, the Neckar basin, they have inherited a tradition, though here of foreign origin, of industrial skill and craftmanship which has been the basis of growth and prosperity in modern times.

Above Mainz, away from the Rhine, stands Darmstadt, on the thickly forested edge of the Odenwald, once the capital of the Grand Duchy of Hesse-Darmstadt, a modern town which owed its initial growth entirely to the presence of the ducal court, but now a centre of the chemical industry. Near by is Goddelau, the birthplace of one of the most gifted and original Germans of the nineteenth century, Georg Büchner. Born in 1813 and dying of typhoid fever in 1837, in his short life he wrote three plays, *Danton's Tod*, *Leonce und Lena*, and *Wozzeck*. They were deeply influenced by Shakespeare and by the poets of the *Sturm und Drang* in Germany; none was produced in his lifetime, but they were to have a profound influence on German expressionism and on the European theatre of the late nineteenth and twentieth centuries. One of them provided the libretto for a modern musical masterpiece, Alban Berg's *Wozzeck*.

Büchner combined a deeply imaginative view of the world with a gift of realism and objectivity which many modern writers have tried to imitate but few have equalled. A medical student, and later a lecturer at the university in Zürich, he wrote a brilliant doctorial thesis on the nerves of the brain, and his interest in scientific experiment and observation recalls that of another great poet of the Rhineland, Goethe. Büchner's death at the age of twenty-four was as great a tragedy for the literature of his own country and of Europe as that of his English contemporary, Keats.

But for those who are interested in the life and character of the people of the Rhine, Büchner's life and personality are no less interesting than his works. Like many young Germans of his time, he responded passionately to the revolutionary movement which was released in Germany by the revolution in Paris in 1830. As a student of Giessen he founded a revolutionary club, *The Society of the Rights of Man*, and wrote and distributed a revolutionary pamphlet, *Der Hessische Landbote* (The Hessian Messenger) which was a violent appeal to the peasants of Hesse to rise against their reactionary princes. For this, he was forced to fly to Strasbourg, where he died.

Büchner's plays, letters, and *obiter dicta* contain passages which are often uncanny anticipations of the views of another great

Rhineland revolutionary, Karl Marx ('There's not much difficulty in being an honourable man if one has soup, meat and vegetables to eat every day.'), only in him they are illuminated by the insight of a poet and by profound sympathy with the condition of his fellow men. Many of the great men of the Rhineland, as for instance in modern times, Adenauer, are striking because of the degree to which they reflect the deep piety, puritanism, conservatism and Catholicism of its people; there are others, like Heine, Büchner and Marx who are no less typical in the degree to which they have revolted against everything which these imply and among them Büchner was as near to genius as any. After the Napoleonic wars, Darmstadt inherited the position which had once belonged to Heidelberg, the capital of the Princes Palatine, who had ruled both banks of the river. Heidelberg, with its marvellous position at the mouth of the Neckar, was once one of the most flourishing centres of German renaissance culture and is still today one of the most attractive of German towns, happily undamaged by the last war. But it was pillaged and reduced to ruins in the wars of Louis xiv and in 1720 the capital of the Palatinate was removed to Mannheim; after the Napoleonic wars the lands of the Palatinate on the left bank of the river were annexed to Hesse-Darmstadt and became part of the Grand Duchy.

Like Heidelberg, like Worms, Speyer also has in modern times declined in importance, as compared with Frankfurt, or with Mannheim, which as a result of the removal of the obstacles to the navigation of the Rhine has become one of the largest inland ports in Europe. Like Heidelberg, Speyer also suffered terrible devastation in the wars of Louis xiv; but its cathedral, with its long line of tombs of the Holy Roman Emperors, who were ceremonially buried there, remain as evidence of its former greatness among the Rhine cities. Speyer, Heidelberg, Worms, Mainz, Frankfurt, are enduring memorials to the extraordinary richness, variety and complexity of the life of the Rhine valley and of the splendours of its past. Their prosperity today, after the immense destruction and suffering caused by the last war, is also evidence of its persistent vitality and an almost miraculous capacity for recuperation. The river as it flows past them, with its immense burden of traffic, carries with it an overpowering weight of memories, of gods and heroes, of saints, knights and emperors, of the rise and fall of great cities, of the piety, the learning, the lusts and ambitions of the Church, of war and peace, of savage devastation, and of life revived where once it had seemed to be totally destroyed. There is perhaps no area in Europe which is so rich in evidence of the continuity, through the most dramatic changes, of the European past. But the rise of modern industry, and especially its renewed efflorescence since the last war, have also transformed the Rhine valley in this area, particularly between Frankfurt and Mainz, into one of the most densely populated and industrially prosperous areas in Europe.

West of Wiesbaden lies the Rheingau, the grape-covered strip of land which extends for fifteen miles at the foot of the mountains to Bingen and is the source of the finest of all the wines of the Rhine. The vineyards that stretch along the river have been cultivated for nearly two thousand years and all the changes, political, military, economic and industrial that have taken place in this area have scarcely changed their character. To the genuine lover of wine this narrow strip of ground is more precious than anything else the Rhine has to offer.

The white wine that comes from these vineyards owes its excellence above all to the delicacy of its bouquet, said to be derived from the free acid which it contains; according to the great German chemist, Liebig, its chemical constituents endow it with health giving properties. Its alcholic content is no higher than 8% or 9%, but it seems to have all the sunshine of the world in it. It is never fortified by brandy or other preservatives, but has excellent keeping properties and sometimes may retain its qualities for up to fifty years, owing to the natural process of fermentation which it undergoes. At its best it has an aroma which makes it the finest of all white wines.

The best of all comes from Schloss Johannisberg; the genuine wine of that name is produced by vineyards of not more than sixty acres in extent, so that very little of it comes onto the open market; it is a wine to be drunk in private and only with those one loves the best. But the other growths of the neighbourhood, known as Johannisberg-Klaus are also of very high quality; again it is the delicacy of their flavour rather than their strength which distinguishes them. The *Johannisberger* which comes from the village of that name is inferior in quality, and indeed is less good than many of the other products of the Rheingau.

The supreme excellence of the best Rhine wine also makes it something of a rarity. The quality of the crop varies greatly from year to year; the best crops only occur on an average ten years in a century. It also varies from district to district, owing to climatic conditions, and this occurs even in the best years. Rhine wine tends to be expensive because the yield of the best vineyards is insufficient to satisfy the world wide demands for their products, whose lightness and delicacy often commend them to people who normally do not like wine. Ghosts are said to drink only the aroma of the wines that are set before them; if this is so, it is surely in the Rheingau that they congregate most willingly.

After Schloss Johannisberg, the finest wines of the Rheingau come from Geisenheim, Rüdesheim, Sternberg, on the slopes behind Hattenheim, Rauenthal, and the Marcobrunn vineyard between Hattenheim and Erbach. Bingen itself is known for its strong wines; below it, on the left bank of the river, is Asmannshausen which produces an excellent red wine, akin to Burgundy, which however does not travel well. The white wines of the Rheingau have come to be known generically as hock, beloved of Byron when diluted with seltzer water; but the name in fact derives from Hochheim, on the Main, which produces a white wine of exceptionally high quality.

The great market for the wines of the Rheingau is Mainz, the centre of the wine trade of the entire Rhine valley and of Germany as a whole; wine has played an important part in the life of the city since it was founded by the Romans. Anyone who wishes to sample any of the over 200 growths of German wine, from the noblest to the humblest, may do so at the *Haus des Deutschen Weines*, founded in 1958 to mark the importance of Mainz to the German wine trade.

Among them, the first place certainly belongs to the wines of the Rheingau, but other areas of the Rhine valley contribute to their variety. Below Bingen, in the Rhine gorge, good white wines are produced at Lorch, Enghöll, Steeg, Oberwesel, and Boppard, while an excellent pale-red wine known as *Rheinbleicherte* is produced at Steeg, Oberwesel and Bacharach, and another light-red wine comes from Salzig, Camp, Horchheim, the Kreuzburg and Urbar, and from below Coblenz. The *Rheinbleicherte* of Linz, near the Drachenfels and the junction of the Rhine and the Ahr, is exceptionally good.

Across the Rhine from Rheingau lies the great wine bearing area of the Palatinate, which greatly surpasses it in the quantity, though not the quality of its products. From Bodenheim, near Worms, the great tourist road known as the *Deutsche Weinstrasse* (the German Wine Road) runs south for sixty miles along the foot of the Hardt mountains through the most productive wine bearing area of Germany. The vineyards at Ruppertsberg, Deidesheim and Forst produce white wine of very good quality; slightly less good is the white wine of Ungstein, Dürckheim, Wachenheim, Konigsbach. Gimmeldingen and Callstadt produce good red wines. The inferior wines of the area tend to be somewhat rough and coarse.

From Rhein-Hesse come the white wines of the vineyard covered hills between Worms and Mainz. These include the excellent *Scharlachberger*, and the only slightly inferior *Niersteiner*, *Oppenheimer*, *Lauberheimer* and *Bodenheimer*, all extremely pleasant wines though less delicate than those of the Rheingau. *Liebfraumilch*, a white wine which perhaps owes its popularity as much to its name as to its drinking qualities, comes from the vineyards near the Gothic church, the *Liebfraukirche*, in a suburb of Worms, but their yield is only sufficient to produce a fraction of the wine which claims the title. Ingelheim between Mains and Bingen produces a good light-red wine and the valley of the Nahe full-bodied white wines that are slightly lacking in flavour.

Above the Nahe, the valley of the Moselle produces light-bodied white wines which, at their best, are distinguished by their delicate and aromatic flavour, though in bad years inclined to be acid. Apart from being delicious, they are recommended for their health-giving qualities. The vineyards lie among rugged slate rocks; the best of the Moselle wines are *Brauneberger*, *Ohligsberger*, *Berncasteler Doctor* which have a particularly fragrant bouquet, and only slightly inferior are *Zeltingen*, *Piesport*, *Graach* and *Grünhaus*. From the Saar valley comes an even lighter but more fully flavoured white wine than those of the Moselle, of which *Schwarzhofberger* is excellent. The most northerly of the vineyards of the Rhineland lie in the valley of the Ahr, above Bonn, which produces a light and pleasant *Ahrbleicherte* which is for the most part consumed locally.

So also are the wines of Baden, with its white and red *Markgräfler*, of the Neckar, and of the Bergstrasse, on the slopes of the Odenwald, near Darmstadt. But all contribute to the great variety of wines, of every quality, which enrich the life of the Rhine. For the wines of the Rhine and its tributaries are not merely of gastronomic importance. The people of the Rhine are by nature and by history wine drinkers and this contributes to giving them something of the pleasure loving and easy going nature of more southern peoples. The bunches of golden grapes which signpost the *Deutsche Weinstrasse* reflect an aspect of the Rhine which is sometimes difficult to remember today amid all the evidence of immense and dynamic industrial activity of which the river is the waterway; but they symbolize an element in the life of the river which has endured for centuries and provide one of the greatest pleasures which the river has to offer.

4 The Rhine Gorge

MOSELLE AND MEUSE

Below Mainz, the Rhine enters on its spectacular myth-and-legend-laden course through the gorge which carries it to the great northern plain that opens out below Bonn. But just as the lands on its right bank down to Mainz are drained by the two great tributaries of the Neckar and the Main, so those on its left bank are drained by two other important tributaries, the Moselle and the Meuse, each of which makes its own particular contribution to the life of the river. There are, however, important differences both historical and geographical, between these two great pairs of tributaries which enter the Rhine from its east and its west bank. Those to the west, the Moselle and the Meuse, are sharply cut off from the Rhine. The mountain line of the Vosges, as compared with the Black Forest, is continuous and unbroken, and between them and the Hardt mountains to the north, there is no easily passable country like the Kraichgau between Karlsruhe and Heidelberg; while the steep, narrow, beautiful valley of the Nahe which enters the Rhine at Bingen is in the sharpest contrast to the broad, highly industrialized plain between the Taunus and the Odenwald through which the Main flows past Frankfurt to meet the Rhine at Mainz.

Further, both the Neckar and the Main join the Rhine within the limits of the Rift valley, before it is blocked by the mountains of the Taunus at its northern end, while both the Meuse and the Moselle cut their way through the great plateau which the Rhine enters above Bingen. Lastly, the Neckar and the Main are, and always have been, completely German rivers, while neither the Meuse nor the Moselle belongs to any single country along the entire length of its course, and control of them has repeatedly changed hands from one state to another.

It was the fate of Lorraine, the area in which the basins of the upper Meuse and Moselle are contained, to form a buffer territory between the states out of which modern France and modern Germany have developed. It was separated from Germany, and the Rhine, by the mountains of the Vosges, the Hardt and the Hunsrück; yet at the same time its natural outlet was towards Germany and away from France, because its navigable rivers flow towards the Rhine and not the Seine. Lorraine suffered the fate of all such buffer territories, in that it was for centuries an area in which the ambitions of its neighbours were at their bitterest and most intense, and the banks of the Meuse and the Moselle are today still scattered with ruins which are a monument to the conflict between them.

Some of the causes of this conflict may be found in the different functions performed by the two rivers in the area which embraces their upper reaches. The Meuse has practically no tributaries, apart from the Chiers and the Semois, which join it as it enters Belgium, and flows directly north for 120 miles from its source through a valley cut into the high ground east of Champagne, from which it is divided by the narrow range of hills which rise to the heights of the Argonne. For centuries, therefore, until France's expansion eastwards towards the Rhine in the sixteenth and seventeenth centuries, it formed what was roughly the boundary between France and Germany. The Moselle, on the other hand, is the central artery of Lorraine, draining it towards the Rhine. Both on its right and its left banks, it receives large tributaries, the Meurthe, the Saar, the Orne, the Sauer, and the most important cities of Lorraine, Nancy, Metz, Trier, stand either on the banks of the Moselle or of its tributary, the Meurthe. The function of the Moselle as a waterway uniting Lorraine with the Rhine is emphasized by the plain of the Bucht von Trier, or Gulf of Trier, which the Moselle projects like a tongue into the high plateau of the Eifel and the Hunsrück west of the Rhine at Coblenz.

The Moselle has always exerted an important strategic influence on the complex history of the lands west of the Rhine, which for many centuries revolved around the three cities of Cologne,

Mainz and Trier. To the Romans, the river formed an essential part of their approach to the Rhine frontier of Gaul; the road from the Mediterranean entered the Moselle valley at Toul, and from there ran through Metz to Trier, where, in the broad green valley among the vineyards, protected by the surrounding heights, and at the mouth of the gorge cut into the bleak plateau, they established a military camp, connected by the river to the Rhine at Coblenz and by a depression across the plateau to the Rhine at Cologne in the north and Bingen in the south.

The administrative divisions of the Roman territories on the Rhine had a decisive influence on their later development. Mainz was the capital of the province of Upper Germany, which included Alsace between the Rhine and the Vosges and, north of the Lauter, Speyer, Worms, the basin of the Nahe and a strip of land on both sides of the Rhine above Coblenz. Cologne was the capital of Lower Germany, which extended north and west of Coblenz and included the basin of the Meuse to beyond Namur. The two provinces were divided by the territory of the province of Upper Belgica, with its capital at Trier, stretching down the Moselle valley almost as far as Coblenz and south and west to the sources of the Meuse and the Moselle; Metz and Trier derive their names from the Gallic tribes of the Mediomatrici and the Treveri, who were established on the Rhine before the coming of the Romans.

The ecclesiastical boundaries on the Rhine in the Middle Ages roughly corresponded to those of the Roman provinces, so that the archbishoprics of Cologne and Mainz were separated by that of Trier, which included the episcopates of Toul, Metz and Verdun and extended beyond Trier on both sides of the Moselle to Coblenz and across the Rhine up the Lahn to Wetzlar and Giessen.

When Charlemagne's empire was divided among his successors, the whole of the Moselle and Meuse basin were included in the great middle kingdom of Lotharingia; when that kingdom was itself sub-divided, Metz, Toul, Verdun, Trier and the Moselle valley down to Coblenz became part of the Duchy of Upper Lotharingia. During the Middle Ages Upper Lotharingia was further fragmented. Metz, Toul, Verdun became free imperial cities, while their bishops ruled the countryside around them. The valley of the Moselle from Trier to Coblenz fell under the rule of the Archbishop of Trier; what remained of Upper Lotharingia became the Duchy of Lorraine, with its capital at Nancy. One of the first steps in France's expansion eastwards towards the Rhine was the transfer to the French crown in the sixteenth century of the archbishoprics of Metz, Toul and Verdun. In the seventeenth century, Alsace and the free city of Strasbourg became French, but the Duchy of Lorraine remained as an independent enclave within French territory, while the valley of the Moselle continued to be ruled from Trier. But here as elsewhere Napoleon put an end to ecclesiastical sovereignty on the Rhine. The Archbishop of Trier removed his seat of government to Coblenz just before the French revolution; when the revolution broke out Coblenz became a refuge and a centre of conspiracy for the emigré French aristocracy. The territories of the archbishop were secularized by Napoleon, and in 1815 the ancient rivalry between Trier and Cologne was ended when both were annexed to Prussia and became part of her Rhine province. The Nahe valley, however, together with Worms and Speyer, preserved its historical relation with the Mainz and Neckar basins across the Rhine; Mainz was annexed to Hesse-Darmstadt, and the area around Speyer and Kaiserslautern to the kingdom of Bavaria.

The Napoleonic wars, from which a new Europe emerged, conferred a new strategic significance on Metz, on the upper Moselle, and the change was emphasized by the development of rail and road communications in the nineteenth century. To the Romans, Metz had merely been the point at which the road from north to south from Trier to Lyons crossed the east-west road from Strasbourg through the Gate of Zabern to the basin of the Seine. Napoleon saw it as a centre of communications commanding the route to the Rhine through the Nahe valley to Mainz, and built a military road, the Kaiserstrasse, connecting the two cities. Until then, the Nahe valley, like Alsace, had belonged naturally to the neighbouring German lands across the Rhine, and the outlets from Lorraine had been either through the Moselle valley to Coblenz or through the Gate of Zabern to Strasbourg.

The strategic importance of Metz, and of the road through the Nahe valley, was increased by the political and industrial development of the nineteenth century. By the European settlement of 1815, France was deprived of the lower Saar valley, above and below Saarbrücken, and it became possible to connect laterally, within Prussian territory, the routes running south-west from the Rhine through the valleys of the Nahe and the Moselle; the lateral road ran through the great coal deposits of the Saar which were developed in the nineteenth century. Both the German annexation of Metz in 1870 and French efforts to detach the Saar from Germany after 1918, were dominated by the desire to control its industrial resources and the routes leading to the Rhine from Metz. The canalization of the Saar river, from Saargemünd to Saarburg, where it crosses the Marne and Rhine canal, made it possible to export the coal of the Saar by water to Strasbourg, and thence by the Rhine-Rhône canal to the industrial area of Colmar and Mulhouse and by rail to south Germany and Switzerland. From 1870 to 1918 the whole of this system of waterways was in German hands. Roads to the Saar converged from Bingen, Mainz, Speyer and Worms, but their importance as Rhine ports was eclipsed by the growth of Ludwigshafen opposite to Mannheim.

The Nahe valley lies between the Hunsrück and the Soonwald and the Westerich, which continues the line of the Hardt Mountains beyond Worms; it is an area of hills whose streams collect to form the Nahe and, around Bad Kreuznach ten miles above Bingen, of volcanic rocks, the outlying edge of the coal deposits of the Saar. Here a group of ruined castles, destroyed by the French in the *annua terribilis* of 1689, perpetuate the memory of the minor feudal lords who dominated the area in the Middle Ages; immediately above Bad Kreuznach, Kauzenberg, the castle of the Counts of Sponheim; three miles higher up, Rheingrafenstein, with the castle of the Rheingrafen, or Counts of the Rhine, dizzily poised four hundred feet above the river; within a mile, the Ebernberg, where in 1520 Franz von Sickingen gave refuge to Ulrich von Hutten; a little higher up, Dhaun, on the steep wooded banks of the Simmer as it comes to join the Nahe through a gorge in the Soonwald. These castles, protected by their position in the hills and woods above the river, were the strongholds of petty barons who warred fiercely with each other and with the ecclesiastical potentates of Trier and Mainz; their lands were later swallowed up in the Palatinate and finally divided between Prussia and Bavaria. Some, however, retained a pale shadow of independence into modern times; the upper valley of the Nahe, on whose steep banks stand the ruins of the castles of the lords of Oberstein, forms the boundary of the little principality of Birkenfeld, which until this century remained a detached possession of the Duchy of Oldenburg.

The Nahe finds its source at the foot of a volcanic hill, the Schaumburg, rising to 2,000 feet, which commands a view of both the Nahe and the Saar valleys and forms the watershed between them. To the south of it is Neunkirchen, on the edge of the densely populated area of the Saar, and beyond Neunkirchen, Saarbrücken, the capital of the area, where the roads and railways converge from Bad Kreuznach up the Nahe valley and from Bad Kreuznach through Kaiserslautern. In the Franco-Prussian war, the right arm of the German army formed up behind Saarbrücken and the decisive battles of the war, concluding in the total encirclement of Metz, were based on the strategic opportunities offered by the communication running through the hilly country in an angle between the bend of the Rhine and the upper Moselle basin.

Metz itself is placed in the angle formed by the Moselle and its tributary the Seille, in a position which, surrounded by hills, was once of great natural strength. Modern artillery, however, can dominate it from the hills, and after the Franco-Prussian war its ramparts were torn down and replaced by a ring of forts with a radius of forty miles. The military significance of Metz in modern times is in sharp contrast with its ecclesiastical importance in the past, of which the enduring memorial is its great cathedral, the rival of Strasbourg and Rheims.

From Metz the Moselle flows north between thickly wooded hills to a few miles above Trier where it is joined, within a few miles of each other, by the Saar on its right bank and the Sauer on its left. Between the two, high on the northern edge of the valley stands the Roman monument of the Heidenturm, or Tower of the Heathen, and beyond is the site of the northern Roman capital of Augusta Trevirorum, which today is Trier or Trèves. Below Trier, the Moselle is joined from the north by the valley of the Kyll, through which ran the Roman road from Cologne, so that the Roman city was placed at a point where the valleys of the upper and the lower Moselle, the Kyll, the Saar and the Sauer all met.

The rectangular town plan of Trier derives from its origin as a military camp, but the sites of Roman villas in the neighbourhood show that it was also a residential area, and for some emperors it was a city which they preferred to Rome. In the fourth century it became the seat of an archbishopric, and thereafter, until the French revolution, was important as an ecclesiastical power; its archbishop was both a sovereign prince and an elector of the empire. In the last war it suffered severely from air attack, and many of its monuments, including its cathedral, were damaged, but the damage has been restored and today Trier, in its green plain surrounded by wooded hills, with its memorials both of Rome and of early Christianity, its red sandstone medieval walls and towers, remains one of the most interesting cities in northern Europe.

Apart from the greatness of its past, and the memorials of it which still remain, Trier has another claim to be remembered in history as the birthplace of Karl Marx. He was born there in 1818 of Jewish parents who had embraced Christianity and had all their children baptized. In his background, Marx was typical of the assimilated Jews of the Rhineland, who had contributed so much to its art, literature and science, and indeed he remained all his life deeply influenced by the ideas of the French enlightenment, to which they largely owed their emancipation. He studied at the universities of Bonn and Berlin, where he became a disciple of Hegel before standing his dialect on its head; but in 1842, true to his own dictum that the problem is not to understand the world but to change it, he gave up philosophy for journalism and became editor of the radical newspaper, the *Rheinische Zeitung*, in Cologne.

Marx's extreme radical views made him obnoxious to the Prussian government. His newspaper was suppressed and he himself was expelled from the Rhineland. He emigrated to Paris where, with Heine, he edited the German language newspaper, *Vorwärts*; from Paris he moved to Brussels where, in *Misère de la Philosophie*, he laid the foundations of the economic interpretations of history, and, on the eve of the February revolution in Paris in 1848, published *The Communist Manifesto*.

The German revolution of 1848 which followed the revolution in France allowed Marx to return to Cologne and revive his newspaper under the title of the *Neue Rheinische Zeitung*. The revolution of 1848 was largely a revolt of West Germany, liberal, bourgeois, industrial and democratic, against the feudal autocracy of Prussia and of the German princes, and it was natural that the first democratic parliament of a united Germany should have been summoned in Frankfurt. The defeat of the revolution was followed by Marx's expulsion, once again, from the Rhineland. He found asylum in London, where he spent the remaining thirty-four years of his life in the deepest poverty and suffering, and in developing the ideas of a social philosophy which was to shake the world.

Marx personified in an extreme form the hostility of his native Rhineland to the hegemony of Prussia, though he also came to reject totally the middle class liberalism which offered itself as an alternative. But in his youth and in his years in Cologne he was not yet the man who wrote *Das Kapital* and founded the International Working Men's Association, and still represented, in their most radical and extreme form, the hopes which the Rhineland placed in a democratic revolution.

Below Trier, the Moselle and its tributary the Saar form the boundary of the Duchy of Luxembourg. The present Duchy represents only a part of the territory which Luxembourg occupied in the Middle Ages, when it included all the high lands between the Moselle and the Meuse which lay between the Duchy of Lorraine and the Duchy of Brabant. The continued existence of the Duchy today is the result of an historical accident. In 1830, when the kingdom of the Netherlands was separated from Belgium, Luxembourg was divided into two parts, of which the northern one, towards the Meuse, went to Belgium, and the southern, towards the Moselle, to the Netherlands. The death of William III in 1890 left the Netherlands without a male heir, and in accordance with the Salic law governing the succession, Luxembourg, as opposed to the Netherlands, passed through the male line to the Duke of Nassau-Weilberg. Today Luxembourg is the only one of the many principalities of the Rhine basin which still preserves an independent existence.

On this section of its course, the Moselle enters the gorge by which it flows to meet the Rhine, perhaps even more striking and beautiful than the gorge of the Rhine itself. Both the river and the gorge perform a series of intricate and elaborate bends and curves, the river tightly gripped between the cliffs of the gorge, and preserving the same winding and tortuous course that it followed when it once flowed high up over the surface of the plateau which divides it from the Rhine. From Trier to Neumagen, once the site of an imperial palace, is a distance of fifteen miles as the crow flies and twenty-two miles by water; from Bernkastel, where the river enters the most tortuous section of the gorge, to Cochem is sixteen miles by land and fifty along the river. Below Neumagen also are the vineyards, and a series of small towns—Piesport, Brauneberg, Bernkastel, Graach, Zeltingen—after which the wines have been named which are one of the great glories of the Moselle, and on the heights above them stand the ruins of castles whose history often illustrates the bitter hostility which once existed between their feudal lords and the archbishops of Trier. At Starkenburg, in the fourteenth century, the archbishop was captured and imprisoned by its countess, who with the ransom he paid for his release built the twin castle of Grafenburg which stands beside it.

THE GORGE

The Moselle enters the Rhine at Coblenz, striking it at right angles to its course through the fifty-mile long gorge which carries it from Bingen to Königswinter, above Cologne. The gorge is the most dramatic and impressive feature in the whole of the Rhine's long and varied journey to the sea, its landscape the most romantic and seductive, bathed in so dense an atmosphere of myth and legend that nowhere on the river is the sense of the past so strong. The river today carries an immense burden both of commercial traffic and pleasure craft, which testify to the prosperity and intense activity of life in the Rhineland. But its banks, and its waters, also carry a different kind of traffic, of water nymphs and witches and sirens and dragons scaled like fishes, of warriors and saints and emperors, of feudal knights and lovesick girls, and nowhere does their presence make itself so immediately felt as on the course of the river through the gorge.

Coblenz is indeed the meeting place of two gorges which at this point cut through the great bleak high-lying plateau which extends along both sides of the Rhine below Bingen; the first is the gorge of the Rhine itself, and the second the gorge of the Moselle, which is continued across the Rhine by the valley of the Lahn. It is also the crossing place of the twin railway lines that run along both banks of the Rhine and the east-west railway running from Berlin and Kassel by the Lahn and Moselle valleys to Metz. As a result of its position, it is the only large town on the banks of the Rhine within the limits of the plateau.

To the south of Coblenz rise the range of the Taunus, on the right bank of the Rhine, and on its left bank the Hunsrück; to the north, across the Moselle, the mountains of the Eifel on the left bank and across the Rhine those of the Westerwald. These four blocks of high land, the more mountainous to the south, compose the single exposed plateau through which the Rhine, the Moselle and the Lahn cut their way. To the south-east, the brink of the Taunus above the forty-mile grape-laden belt of the Rheingau is steep and thickly wooded, while its northern slope into the valley of the Lahn is more gradual. The southern face of the Hunsrück is less steep than that of the Taunus, but its northern edge, as it falls into the valley of the Moselle, also forms an easy and gradual slope. From both ranges the streams drain not into the Rhine but into its tributaries, the Lahn and the Moselle, so that from Bingen to Coblenz the face of the Rhine gorge is continuous and unbroken.

The entry of the Rhine into the gorge at Bingen is perhaps the most dramatic spectacle along the whole length of the river. Above Bingen, the Rhine is up to a thousand yards wide, flowing between low banks and divided by a series of long wooded islands which obscure the outlook ahead. In the distance are the mountains of the Taunus and the Hunsrück, which gradually draw closer together until they present an almost continuous face broken only by the narrow opening between the opposing cliffs. Through this, compressed between the steep banks, the Rhine pours with a swift and powerful current to the Binger Loch, an artificial channel dug in the bed of the river, over what were once rapids obstructed by rocks which were removed in order to make navigation easier. Modern engineering has greatly improved navigation in the gorge; but the many legends of shipwrecks that have taken place in its treacherous waters, in which heroes, saints and emperors have been involved and sometimes only saved by divine intervention, show what a hazard they once were to the sailor.

In the gorge the banks are vine-clad on their lower slopes, their rocks dark and sombre in colour, rising steeply to the level heights of the plateau and revealing at every bend of the river some small town or village huddled at the foot of castle ruins poised upon the crags above; rocks, woods, skies that are sometimes brilliant and blue and sometimes overhung by mist, the dark green swiftly flowing waters of the river, vineyards, ruins, brilliant contrasts of light and shadow, golden sunshine on the dark-faced walls of the gorge, wide-winged birds that seem to fall from the mountains above, all combine to create an impression which is at once brilliant and sombre, savage and serene; the impression indeed which is precisely what we mean by romanticism.

Bingen itself, an ancient little town of Gallo-Roman origin, lies in the angle formed by the river Nahe and the Rhine, at the point where the Rhine sweeps into the gorge, beneath the Rochusberg and the castle of Klopp, the site of what was once a Roman fortress; the seven-arched bridge across the Nahe is also built on Roman foundations. Across the Rhine is the ruined castle of Rheinfels, and on an island in the river at the mouth of the gorge, is the Mausturm, or Mouse Tower where the ill-famed Archbishop Hatto was eaten by rats. In the Middle Ages, Bingen was a free city and a member of the Rhenish League; the legends associated with the Archbishops of Mainz, mostly to their discredit, reflect the bitter hostility of the citizens and peasants to the temporal ambitions of the Church.

From Bingen to Coblenz, the forty miles of the gorge, dark-walled and precipitous, are unbroken, and the little towns at the foot of the cliffs and the castles on the heights above them follow each other as in some marvellous tapestry woven out of the history of the river. Facing each other like two rivals across the Rhine are Rheinfels and Ehrenbreitstein, once the residences of the archbishops of Trier and Mainz. Below them, on the right bank, are the ruins of Falkenburg and Sooneck, fortresses from which robber lords raided the medieval traffic on the river. At Lorch, at the mouth of the valley of the Wisper, legend says that a knight once rode his horse straight up the precipitous cliffs to the castle of Nollich on its summit. Below Lorch lies what was once the territory of the Counts Palatine of the Rhine, and the two little towns of Bacharach and Caub, the first overlooked by the three ruined castles of Fürstenberg, Stahleck and Stahlberg, and the second by Gutenfels, while on a rocky island between them are the ruins of the castle of Pfalz. Bacharach has two beautiful churches, one a round Romanesque temple, the other Gothic; beyond it, on the left bank of the river, in the little town of Oberwesel, are the ruins of the castle of Schonburg. All these ruins are memorials to the terrible destruction carried out by the French in the single year of 1689.

Three miles below Oberwesel, past the menacing rock of the Lorelei, the river enters what was once the territory of the Counts of Katzenelnbogen, perhaps the most impressive stretch in the whole gorge. St Goar, on the left bank, with the ruins of the castle of Rheinfels, and St Goarshausen, on the right bank, with with those of Neu Katzenelnbogen, secured for their owners command of the tolls imposed on the medieval traffic on the river. The castle of Neu Katzenelnbogen was known as the Cat, to match the other castle of the Mouse further down the river;

beyond it are the castles of Sterrenberg and Liebenstein, which belong to the Archbishop of Trier, and beyond them the little town of Boppard, once like Oberwesel a free imperial city which prospered from the Rhine traffic. Here the river makes a great double bend, past the castle of Marksburg, another possession of the Katzenelnbogen, five hundred feet above the river, which escaped destruction by the French and survived to serve as a state prison until annexed by Prussia in 1886.

Beyond, on the right bank, is the Königstuhl, once a meeting place for the four electors of the Rhine whose lands adjoined them. Rhens, above it, on the right bank, belonged to Cologne; Kapellen, below it, to Trier; Lahnstein, across the river from Kapellen, to Mainz; Caub and Bacharach to the Counts Palatine of the Rhine. Below the Königstuhl, near Coblenz, high on the left bank of the river, is the castle of Stolzenfels, 300 feet above the river and commanding a magnificent view. It was once a fortress and residence of the Archbishops of Trier. Destroyed by the French in 1698, it was rebuilt by the Emperor Frederick William IV as a Rhineland residence, in Romantic Neo-Gothic, for the Hohenzollerns. Below Stolzenfels, on the right bank, is a small delta formed by the Lahn as it enters the Rhine, flowing under the first bridge below Mainz. Immediately beyond the bridge is Ehrenbreitstein on the right bank, and Coblenz on the left.

No reach of the river so well illustrates and exemplifies the complexities of the historical development of western Germany as its course through the gorge from Bingen to Coblenz. The narrowness of the gorge, which allows little room for development on its banks, and the absence of any important tributaries, have inhibited the growth of any large cities, while the small towns which depend on the peaceful traffic of the river were continually at the mercy of the feudal overlords—Mainz, Trier, the Counts Palatine, Cologne, Katzenelnbogen—who seized a frontage on the Rhine in order to secure a share of the tolls exacted from its shipping. None of these feudal powers were strong enough to establish a predominent position; each was strong enough to prevent the domination of another. Both their strength and their weakness combined to make their rivalries bitter and enduring. It was not until after Napoleon had suppressed them that, in 1815, the gorge became a boundary between Nassau on the right bank, and, on the left bank, Hesse from Mainz to Bingen and Prussia from Bingen to Coblenz, so that a measure of order and stability was introduced into the political confusion that had ruled in the gorge for so many centuries.

The evidence of that confusion is to be seen in the number and variety of the feudal strongholds that line the banks of the gorge and that even today lends so varied a charm to its landscape. That charm is enhanced by the wealth of legends, pagan, Roman and Christian, which have attached themselves to this stretch of the Rhine, and allow one to see, as in a glass darkly, how history has mirrored itself in the imagination of poets and of people. *Region de trentes peuples, et de trente siècles*; a region of thirty peoples and of thirty centuries; there is really not much exaggeration in Victor Hugo's description of the gorge.

Coblenz itself, like the Coblenz of Switzerland a 'confluence' of rivers, of Roman origin, then a city of the Franks, later a member of the Rhenish Confederation, centre of conflict in the Thirty Years War, victorious in the French seige of 1688, capital and residence of the archbishops of Trier before the French revolution, nest of emigré conspiracy after its outbreak, devastated in the Second World War, later the capital of the French zone of occupation in Germany, now a shining, prosperous modern city, might well be taken as a symbol of the extraordinary historical vicissitudes and of the enduring vitality of this stretch of the Rhine.

It lies sunk in a small plain where the gorge opens for a short distance between Coblenz and Neuwied; immediately opposite is the citadel of Ehrenbreitstein, with a view that commands the Rhine to north and south, the valley of the Nahe, and, over the plain, the volcanic conical hills of the Eifel. At the northern edge of the plain, the river Wied creeps in through the plateau, past the ruined castle of the Counts of Wied and their country residence of Mon Repos, to join the Rhine at Neuwied, which had the distinction after the Thirty Years War of providing the

Catholic Rhineland a refuge for dissenting sects of every kind, but in particular the Moravian Brothers.

Below Neuwied the gorge opens out, its rocky face broken by fissures caused by volcanic action and by the entrances made by small tributaries on both banks. Andernach, on the right bank, with its medieval towers and walls, just below the entry of the little river Nette, repeats the pattern of many of the small towns of the gorge; Roman, Frankish, free city, subjugated by the Archbishop of Cologne, burned by the French in 1688. Below it are the ruins of the castles of Hammerstein and Rheineck, poised above rocks of black basalt which were quarried, and sent down the Rhine, to build the dykes of Holland. These basalt rocks were the result of volcanic action, which was also responsible for the medicinal springs of Apollinaris, near Remagen, below the delta of the Ahr, named after St Apollinaris, Bishop of Ravenna, whose head was sent down the Rhine as a present to the Archbishop of Cologne, was miraculously halted on its journey and now rests in the marvellous Romanesque church which bears his name. Here the gorge comes to its final and in some way most impressive reach. On the left bank are the volcanic hills of the Rodenberg, on the right the Siebengebirge, and between them the island of Nonnenwerth, the hills thickly wooded and their lower slopes laden with vineyards.

Seen from afar, from the plain to the north, the heights at the mouth of the Rhine gorge stand out like the gates to some distant and mysterious country, and it seems natural that for centuries they have been invested with the enchantments of myth and legend. Above the island of Nonnenwerth is Rolandseck; the hero after whom it is named makes the gorge resound with the echoes of Roncesvalles and the trumpet calls of the *Chanson de Roland*. Across the river is the Drachensfels, the Dragon's Rock, the highest point in the Siebengebirge; from its summit one can see the twin spires of Cologne cathedral, made of the same stone as the rock itself. Near by, in the valley, are the ruins of the great abbey of Heisterbach, destroyed at the beginning of the nineteenth century, which once proved the most appropriate of settings for the magnificent collection of early German paintings which is now one of the great treasures of the Pinakothek at Munich; above it is the Petersberg with its ancient chapel, and beyond it Königswinter, facing Bad Godesberg, ill-famed as the scene of the negotiations between Hitler and Chamberlain which led to the Munich agreement.

The hills which extend north-east and north-west from the gorge of the Rhine below the Lahn and the Moselle are lower than the Hunsrück and the Taunus and have no continuous or conspicuous crest like those two ranges; beginning not far from the bank of the Rhine a little below Coblenz, they form an angle which encloses the extension of the northern plain which projects south along the river past Cologne and Bonn.

On the east of the Rhine, the Westerwald stretches across the Rothaar ridge into the Sauerland; this belt of high land, rising to 3,000 feet at its edge in the Sauerland, forms a watershed from which the Ruhr, the Sieg and the Wied flow north-west towards the Rhine, the Eder south-east to the Weser, and the Lahn first east, then south, then west to the Rhine at Coblenz.

The Lahn, after turning south, emerges completely from the high ground to enter the depression which is connected by the Wetterau to Frankfurt and the upper Rhine valley; here it passes the two rival university towns of Marburg and Giessen, founded by the two ducal houses of Hesse-Kassel and Hesse-Darmstadt. At Giessen the Lahn turns west to cut a deep valley through the Rhine plateau, and roads converge from north, east and south to follow the river to the Rhine. Below Giessen is Wetzlar, the seat of the *Reichsgerichtshof,* or imperial court of justice, after the devastation of Speyer by Louis xiv; it has a greater claim to immortality as the birthplace of a literary creation which inflamed and transformed the imagination of all Europe, for it was here that the young Goethe wrote *The Sorrows of Werther.*

If *Werther* conferred immortality on Wetzlar, it transformed Goethe overnight into a great European figure. In 1774, when it was published, he was twenty-five and had already written one masterpiece, *Gotz von Berlingen.* His novel was the direct product of his experiences in Wetzlar. It was there that he had fallen in love and been rejected, and there that a friend who was also a poet and in love had committed suicide. But the despair that these experiences inspired in the young Goethe was not a merely personal one; it had in it all the elements of morbidity, cynicism and disillusion which were something new to the sensibility of Europe. *Werther* elevated the sufferings of the individual into a cosmic principle and soon Europe was thronged with brooding, suicidal lovers who saw themselves as the victims of the *Zeitgeist*. Even Napoleon was among them.

That such a revolution in sensibility should have found its origin in the little provincial German town of Wetzlar is an astonishing mark of Goethe's genius; and Goethe himself, in his early years, is one of the most astonishing, perhaps the most astonishing, manifestations of the genius of the Rhineland. From his pedantic and severe father, the Imperial Councillor of Frankfurt, he acquired his linguistic and scientific interests; from his mother, gay, impulsive and lovable, like so many Rhineland women, his love of the popular ballads, tales and legends in which the river abounded. Frankfurt itself brought him into contact with French culture and the French classical theatre; but also with the fairs, marionettes, imperial ceremonials, which were a part of the city's most ancient inheritance. No child had a richer or more varied cultural heritage. After three years in Leipzig, which he described as a small Paris, he continued his studies at Strasbourg; but law was of less importance to him than the influence of Herder, whose belief in the insufficiency of reason, in the importance of myth and folk tale as the expression of the soul of a race and a people was one of the factors which finally decided him to be a German rather than a French writer. Equally important was yet another love affair, with Frederike Brion, daughter of the pastor of the little village of Sesenheim, up the river from Strasbourg. Of the village, which was destroyed in the last war, nothing remains except the gravestone of Frederike's father. Frederike has her memorial in Goethe's poems to her, in the simplicity of his pastoral idyll *Hermann und Dorothea*, most of all in the immense drama of *Faust*, which certainly had its inception in the days when Goethe travelled the roads of Alsace. All this Goethe already had behind him when he went to Wetzlar and before he wrote *Werther* and Karl August came to Frankfurt to take him away to his little court at Saxe-Weimar; and is is not fanciful to see in everything he wrote in those days of his wonderful youth, the freshness and the turbulence of the river itself. After Wetzlar it was never quite the same again; Goethe may have become a greater man and a greater poet, but he had ceased to belong to the Rhineland.

Between Wetzlar and its junction with the Rhine at Lahnstein, the Lahn falls from five hundred to two hundred feet above sea level, through many locks and a landscape which is equal to that of the Moselle in natural beauty and romantic association. Limburg, below Giessen, climbs the narrow streets from the water's edge up the steep hill to the foot of the cathedral, one of the most remarkable in Germany, seven-towered and built in a style which marks the transition from Romanesque to Gothic, and beyond Limburg the heights above the river are crowned by a series of castles, Diez, Oranienstein, Balduinstein, Laurenberg, Ahnstein and Nassau, looking down over the woods in the valley, all the possessions of the house of Nassau, which ruled this marvellous stretch of the river from the Middle Ages until 1866. Near Nassau also are two castles belonging to the family of the great Friedrich von Stein, who laid the foundations of modern Prussia after its defeat at the battle of Jena. Four miles below Nassau is Bad Ems, where a little river enters the Lahn; sunk deep in the valley between the woods that rise to the summits of the Mahlberg and the Bäderlei, its warm springs made its fortune as a fashionable watering place, from the days of the Romans, who included it within the Pfahlgraben, to those of Bismarck, who there gave to the French ambassador Benedetti the reply which made the Franco-Prussian War inevitable.

As the Westerwald fills the angle formed by the Rhine and the Lahn below Coblenz, so the Eifel fills that between the Rhine and the Moselle; nearest the Rhine, around Andernach and Remagen are the Hohe Eifel, where they are at their highest, some thirty miles to the north the Schnee Eifel with their heavy falls of snow, to the south towards the Moselle the volcanic hills of the Vorder Eifel, and to the north the Vorder Venn, which forms a high ridge stretching from south-west to north-east overlooking Aachen and the whole of the northern plain. Through this quadrilateral of high land, in valleys which form an almost continuous passage through them, flow the two beautiful rivers of the Ahr, which joins the Rhine at Remagen, and the Kyll, which joins the Moselle below Trier. From the watershed between them, a third small stream, the Erft, flows north parallel to the Rhine past Bonn and Cologne, until it turns east to join the Rhine at Düsseldorf. The Romans made use of these valleys to construct a road through the Eifel from Cologne along the Erft and the Kyll to join the Moselle at Trier.

Where the Ahr joins the Rhine at Remagen the cliffs form a basalt wall nearly 1,000 feet high; on their summit is the fortress of Landskron and below it the springs of Apollinaris. Up the valley are Neuenahr and Ahrweiler, at the mouth of a deep and tortuous ravine; still higher up is Altenahr, in a marvellous position surrounded by woods rising to a ruined castle on a height that rises to over eight hundred feet. The road through the valley climbs to the foot of the Hohe Acht and the Nurberg, both over 2,000 feet, the highest points of the Hohe Eifel.

The Roman road from Cologne to Trier continues from the Erft up the Kyll valley, past the remains of Roman villas and the two beautifully situated little towns of Gerolstein and Kyllburg, at the foot of thickly wooded limestone cliffs from which castle ruins look down into the river. Between the Kyll valley and the Rhine lies the plateau of the Vorder Eifel, with its strange conical hills cratered by extinct volcanoes and almost perfectly circular lakes where volcanic eruptions blew off the summits of the mountains; the most remarkable of these volcanic remains are the Mosenberg, with four craters in line and a river of lava petrified on its southern slopes, and the lake of Laach, not far from the Rhine at Andernach, an almost perfect circle of five miles in circumference, surrounded by five extinct volcanoes, wooded down to the water's edge and to the marvellous domed and towered abbey of Laach, an architectural monument in a singularly beautiful setting that rivals and perhaps surpasses anything to be found even at Worms, or Speyer, or Trier.

5 The Lower Rhine

THE GERMAN PLAIN

Beyond Bad Godesberg and Königswinter, the Rhine, emerging from its gorge, leaves the mountain ranges which have been its companions all the way from its Alpine sources and enters the great northern plain through which it accomplishes its final journey to the sea. On the southern edge of the plain, the mountains of the Rhine plateau stretch east of the Meuse past Aachen and across the river, bend north to beyond Cologne and then east through the Sauerland to the ridge of the Eggegebirge, from which the hills of the Teutoburgerwald project sixty miles into the plain of Westphalia. Thus, on either side of the river, the plain, like a sea washing into a rocky coast, cuts two deep indentations into the mountains; in the centre of one is Cologne and of the other Münster. The whole of this area is now included in the West German federal state of Nordrhein-Westfalen, and on the banks of the Rhine itself, and of its tributaries, the Ruhr and the Wupper, contains one of the greatest concentrations of industrial power in the world.

On its southern edge the plain does not have the uniform monotony that it does further north; the ground gently rises and falls on both sides of the river, and to the east along the foot of the Sauerland is a belt of hilly country which meets the plain between the Ruhr and the Lippe, flowing west on parallel courses to meet the Rhine. The valley of the Lippe lies within the plain itself, and that of the Ruhr within the hills, and between them is an area which for over a century has been the main source of Germany's industrial strength, providing a major part of the means with which she has waged two world wars, and today has re-established herself as a world industrial power. There is no part of the Rhine basin, or indeed of Germany, which has been of greater significance in the history of modern Europe, and of the world; for that reason it was the primary target of the Allied air attack during the Second World War.

South of the Ruhr, two other rivers rise in the Sauerland and flow north-west through deeply incised valleys in the hills; the Lenne, which joins the Ruhr above Dortmund, and the Wupper, which from north-west makes a complete turn to west, then south, then south-west to join the Rhine between Cologne and Düsseldorf. On its north-westerly reach, it once formed part of the boundary between the Duchy of Lotharingia and the Duchy of Saxony, that is, between the territories of the Franks and the Saxons, and later between Prussia's Rhine province and Westphalia, but today its significance as a frontier has been lost as a result of the reorganization of Germany after the Second World War.

From the Middle Ages down to the French revolution, the basin of the lower German Rhine was divided between four principalities whose lands lay alongside each other parallel to the course of the river. On the left bank, above and below Cologne were those of the Archbishop of Cologne; to the west of it, in the valley of the Roer, flowing north-west between Cologne and Aachen to join the Meuse, lay the Duchy of Jülich. On the right bank, as far as the Saxon frontier, was the Duchy of Berg, and east of it, within Saxony, the County of Mark. North of these territories, on both banks of the river, lay the Duchies of Cleves and of Gelders; on the upper reaches of the Ruhr and the Lippe were the Duchy of Westphalia and the Bishopric of Paderborn, and in the arm of the Teutoburgerwald the Bishopric of Münster. Lying across the Teutoburgerwald were the little lordships of Ravensburg and Minden; in the seventeenth century they became the possessions together with Cleves and Mark of the Elector of Brandenburg and thus formed the nucleus of Prussia's future provinces in Westphalia and the Rhineland. After the defeat of Napoleon, Jülich, Cologne, Berg, the Archbishopric of Trier, Cleves and Gelders were consolidated into the Rhine province; Minden and Ravensburg were added to the Bishoprics of Münster and Paderborn, the ecclesiastical duchy of Westphalia and the County of Mark, to form the province of Westphalia. For fifty years, between 1815 and 1866, these two provinces formed an extension of Prussia in the Rhine Basin.

In the second half of the nineteenth century, the rapid industrial development of the Ruhr valley, in the hills at the foot of the Sauerland, entirely transformed both the physical features of the area and its economic and political significance. From the edge of the high plateau of the Rhine gorge a rich belt of coal-bearing strata extends northwards under the plain, so that even under the bed of the river Lippe coal can be mined at great depth. The coal-field also extends westwards across the Rhine towards Krefeld and München-Gladbach on its left bank, and the river itself has been one of the main routes by which its coal has been exported. The importance of the coalfield was increased by the rich deposits of iron ore in the Lahn and Moselle valleys west of the Rhine. The proximity of almost inexhaustible coal deposits, the primary source of industrial power in the nineteenth and early twentieth centuries, to supplies of iron ore made what is today Nordrhein-Westfalen, that is the basin of the Rhine below Cologne, the centre of the German coal, iron and steel industries, creating a dense belt of population on the southern edge of the plain which is in the sharpest contrast to the thinly populated highlands of the Rhine plateau overlooking it. The iron and steel industry of the Ruhr has in modern times made this part of the Rhine basin one of the decisive industrial and strategic areas, not merely of Europe, but of the world.

Geographically and historically, the natural capital of this stretch of the Rhine is Cologne, and perhaps no city on the river better illustrates, in the most dramatic and varied form, the vicissitudes of history. Under the Roman Empire, it already enjoyed the privileges of a colonial capital, and its geographical position made it one of the great cities of northern Europe. Even before the Christian era, it was the meeting place of four important land and water routes; the Rhine itself, though then the river was narrower than it is today, and its passage obstructed by an island which is now incorporated into the city itself; the great Roman frontier road along the left bank of the river; the road east from the Meuse along the edge of the highlands through

Aachen; the road from Trier and the south along the valley of the Kyll and across the Rhine plateau. The site of the city had the further advantage that here the Rhine makes a wide sweep to the west, offering deep water on the left or Roman bank.

The city had a religious as well as a military and commercial importance. The German tribes which occupied the right bank were compelled by the Romans to cross the river and establish their national altar at Cologne; it is fascinating to reflect that the immense ecclesiastical authority which Cologne has exercised in Christian times should have had its origin in the altars of savages, pagans and heathens. The city became the capital of the Roman province of Lower Germany, as Mainz was of Upper Germany, and Trier of Upper Belgica; and when the Romans were converted to Christianity, Cologne like Mainz and Trier became the seat of a bishopric. Even after the fall of the Empire, when the Franks established themselves on the left bank of the Rhine, Cologne maintained its position as the chief city of the Lower Rhine.

When Charlemagne made Aachen, west of the Rhine, his provincial capital, Cologne became the natural base from which to mount and maintain his expeditions against the Saxons across the river, and equally the ecclesiastical centre of his territories on its left and its right bank. The city was raised to an archbishopric and here as elsewhere along the Rhine the Church tried to establish its temporal as well as spiritual authority on its banks. In the Middle Ages, however, the archbishops were compelled to recognize Cologne as a free city of the Empire and in consequence removed their residence to Bonn.

As a free city, Cologne became a member of the Hanseatic League and enjoyed political privileges and a commercial prosperity which made it a rival to Lübeck for its leadership. The city was the meeting point at which traffic up the river from the sea and down the river from Lake Constance unloaded its cargoes for land transport across the plain, west to Aachen and Flanders and north through Westphalia to Lübeck and the Baltic. Down traffic carried the merchandise of Italy and the Indies; from the sea came that of England. The English trade was so important that the merchants of Cologne maintained their own agency in London next to the Guildhall. Out of the wealth of the traffic of the river came the great medieval foundation which embellished the city, and in particular its cathedral, one of the greatest of all Gothic monuments, begun in 1248, but not finally completed until six centuries later.

This great period of affluence, in which the arts, learning and religion flourished on the produce of trade, was brought to an end by the Reformation. The river traffic from the sea was cut off by the Protestant Netherlands; the Protestants of Cologne were expelled from the city and took their industrial skills with them to neighbouring towns like Deutz, Krefeld, Elberfeld and Düsseldorf. Cologne lost its commercial predominance, and with its great cathedral, its hundred churches and many monastic foundations, which earned it the title of the German Rome, retained only its significance as a centre of religion and ecclesiastical administration.

Commerce and industry entered a new period of expansion in the nineteenth century, after 1815, when Cologne became the capital of Prussia's newly formed Rhine province, and freedom of navigation was restored on the Rhine. After the Franco-Prussian war of 1870 it achieved even greater prosperity as a result of the rapid development of the coalfields east and west of the Rhine, particularly the Ruhr. Railways also gave it increased importance as the junction of the main line from Paris to Berlin and from England and the Netherlands to Italy and Vienna.

But the Second World War brought to Cologne what seemed for a time to be irretrievable disaster. The damage caused by Allied air attack was so extensive that it was even thought that the city could never be rebuilt on its existing site. By 1945 its population had been reduced from 800,000 to 40,000; of 252,000 units of living accomodation in the city, only 20,000 remained. It seemed as if, of the entire city, only the cathedral had, as by a miracle, survived. Anyone who visited Cologne in May 1945 might have been forgiven for thinking that as a city it had ceased to exist. Nevertheless, today, Cologne, rebuilt, is once again a great city, with a population of 850,000, and is still, with its fairs, its carnival, its magnificent medieval monuments, its own particular air in which Catholic piety goes hand in hand with commerce, one of the most interesting towns in northern Europe.

The miracle by which Cologne, and western Germany as a whole, rose like a phoenix out of the ashes of defeat, is one of the most remarkable phenomena of modern history; it was very largely the work of one of Cologne's most remarkable sons, Konrad Adenauer. He was born in Cologne in 1874, and in the course of his long life has surmounted all the kaleidoscopic political changes which Germany has suffered during his lifetime. A child of the Empire of Bismarck and the Hohenzollerns, he survived its fall, the Weimar Republic, the National-Socialist dictatorship, the catastrophe of 1945, Allied occupation, and emerged triumphantly to form his own independent German state orientated not towards Prussia but towards the West.

In 1906 he entered the Cologne city council and from 1917 to 1933 was its *Oberbürgmeister* or mayor, an office which carries much greater power and authority than it does in any English city. In his conduct of the city's affairs he displayed the same autocratic temperament which he showed, over forty years later, as Chancellor of the German Federal Republic; but he did much to encourage the growth and prosperity of the city, reformed and expanded the university, and endowed Cologne with parks, open spaces, sports grounds and public buildings.

On the collapse of the monarchy in 1918, he would have liked to found an autonomous Rhineland as part of a German federal state. He played only a minor part in the politics of Weimar, as a member and later speaker of the Prussian Landtag. Under Hitler he was dismissed from his office of Mayor, and twice arrested. After Germany's defeat, he was reappointed by the British occupation authorities and again dismissed, partly because his dream of rebuilding Cologne on a new site seemed to them utopian and unrealistic.

Thus Adenauer only began his career as a national and international statesman when he was over seventy and became chairman of the newly founded Christian Democratic Union. The CDU was to form the ruling party in every government of the

Federal Republic, of which Adenauer became its first Chancellor on its foundation in 1947, and he remained its undisputed master until his retirement, at the age of eighty-five, fifteen years later.

Adenauer's immense achievement as a statesman was to preside over the foundation of a liberal, democratic and constitutional West German state, to give it firm and stable foundations, to lead it into the closest association with Western Europe, and to help to heal the centuries old conflict between Germany and France. No other post-war statesman has played so productive and creative a role, for Adenauer has the right to be regarded both as the founder of the German Federal Republic and one of the chief architects of the European Economic Community, within which West Germany has found an immense material prosperity and a regained dignity and self respect.

No doubt Adenauer's great achievement reflects his own very remarkable personality, arbitrary, domineering and overbearing, often sly and devious in his tactics, immensely tenacious of political power; but it also reflects a wide and philosophic vision of the new Germany and of the new Europe he helped to create. In this vision the historical traditions and attitudes of the Rhineland have played a decisive part. Geographically, the European Economic Community, of which the Rhineland is the economic centre, corresponds closely with the great empire of which Charlemagne dreamed, with its axis on the Rhine. West Germany itself is essentially a Rhineland state and essentially a Catholic state. Most of all, perhaps, it represents, both in its political structure and its alignment with Western Europe, a revulsion against the centralized, nationalist and militarist form of the state as it evolved in Prussia. It is significant that the determination with which Adenauer led Germany into Western Europe was equalled by his refusal to admit any compromise with the German Democratic Republic which grew out of the destruction of Prussia, even though this might involve the indefinite postponement of any prospect of German reunification. In such attitudes, Adenauer may be regarded as the true representative of his native land.

Cologne, of course, was not alone as a victim of the destruction which descended like fire from heaven on the Rhineland during the Second World War; for the destruction and occupation of the Ruhr was a primary objective, perhaps *the* primary objective, of Allied strategy. In a sense it could be said, that, from a military point of view, the Ruhr *was* Germany, for without the Ruhr Germany ceased to be a major military power. At the end of the war, the industrial areas of the Rhineland looked as if they had been reduced to *tabula rasa*, and as if the principles of total war had been carried out with a thoroughness which the Romans had never been able to achieve with their *delenda est Carthago*.

Rebuilt and restored, this area has today found a new and dazzling industrial prosperity in the affluent world of post-war Germany; nowhere is the evidence of the *Wirtschaftswunder* more apparent than on the waters of the Rhine. Yet beneath the prosperity there are also reasons for anxiety. Coal, which provided the original base for the industrialization of the Ruhr, is today, here as throughout the world, a declining industry, and the future of the coal industry is one of West Germany's unsolved problems. The grimy little mining towns of the Ruhr valley are becoming depopulated as a result of the attractions of the large cities, which have become the centres of new industries, like chemicals, and can offer all the attractions of modern urban life.

Although Cologne has captured much of its former position, it has in some respects declined in importance. Like Frankfurt, Cologne was rejected as a possible capital of the new Federal Republic and the political life of West Germany is concentrated in the neighbouring town of Bonn, higher up the river. Like Cologne a Roman foundation, the residence of the archbishops of Cologne, birthplace of Beethoven, seat of a distinguished university, rich in historical and architectural monuments, Bonn has many claims to distinction, but few if any of the amenities of a capital city, unless political gossip is to be counted among them, and an air of complacent provincialism which its new status as the capital of West Germany, or its new government buildings on the banks of the Rhine, have done nothing to alter. Even its climate has a notoriously enervating effect; the contrast between the feverish and ebullient activity of Germany's industrial cities and

1 In the Grisons, at the sources of the Rhine; the Vorder Rhein as it descends from Lake Toma, at the foot of the Piz Badus

2 In the valley of the Hinter Rhein, as the stream winds down to meet the Vorder Rhein

5   Aerial view of Basle, in the bend of the Rhine between the Jura and the
Black Forest

3   (*opposite above*) Säckingen, between Constance and Basle. The covered
wooden bridge dates from the sixteenth century

4   (*opposite below*) Basle, the Gateway to Switzerland, where the Rhine
leaves Switzerland for Germany. Basle is Switzerland's only port

6 Arrival of St Ursula at Basle, on her return from Rome in company with the Pope, by Hans Memling

7 Strasbourg, capital of Alsace, with the cathedral of Notre-Dame. In the last hundred years, Strasbourg has changed hands four times between France and Germany

8 The Petit-France quarter of Strasbourg, with the fifteenth-century spire of the cathedral in the background

9 The Romanesque cathedral at Speyer, built by the Emperors Conrad III and Henry III between 1030 and 1061 and reconstructed by the Emperor Henry IV from 1082–1125

10 (*opposite*) Siegfried's Corpse, as seen by the nineteenth-century painter, Thomas Pixis. Siegfried was treacherously killed by Hagen while hunting in the forest near the Nibelung capital at Worms

11 The great river port of Mannheim, on the right bank of the Rhine at the junction with the Main, and facing Ludwigshafen

12 Mannheim, with the docks lying between the Neckar and the Rhine, and the eighteenth-century grand-ducal palace

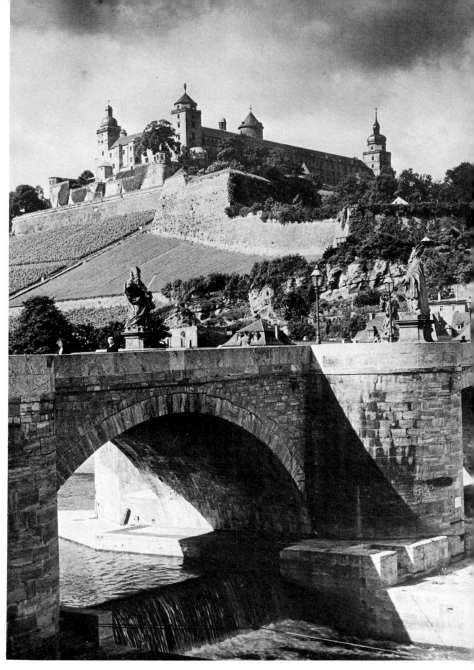

13 The fifteenth-century bridge at Wurzburg, on the Main, leading to the castle of the Marienburg, one of the oldest fortified palaces in Germany

14 Wine harvest at Diedesheim, at the foot of the Hardt mountains between Worms and Speyer. The grapes are being crushed in a portable mangle
15 The Maüseturm, or Mousetower, on an island at the mouth of the Rhine gorge, where the wicked Bishop Hatto was devoured by rats

16 An old engraving of Bacharach, below Brügen, at the mouth of the valley of the Steeg, with the Gothic chapel of St Werner and on the near-side the castle of Stahleck
17 Bacharach today, showing the ruins of St Werner and the thirteenth-century church of St Peter, recently restored

18   The castle of Pfalz, built on the rock of Pfalzgrafenstein in the middle of the Rhine above Kaub, in order to extract tolls from the river traffic

19   In the gorge of the Rhine at the medieval town of Oberwesel with its ancient houses and eighteen crenellated towers. Oberwesel is one of the most picturesque places on the Rhine

20　The Maidens of the Rhine, as seen by the French painter Fantin-
Latour in his illustrations to the *Rheingold*

21 The castle of Katz, built in 1382 above St Goarshausen, as it appeared to the nineteenth-century English illustrator, Habillot Browne

22 The fortress of Rheinfels, above St Goar, now in ruins

23   The castle of Rolandseck, below Bonn, with the island of Nonnenwerth below, and facing the rock of the Drachenfels

24   Logging on the Rhine, in the shadow of the Lorelei. The timber is cut when the snows melt, and floated down the Rhine

25. The Romanesque cathedral of Trier, on the Moselle. Trier is the most ancient city in Germany, with important Roman, Medieval and Baroque remains, but is today an active manufacturing and commercial city, and the centre of the wine trade of the Moselle

26   Karl Marx, born in 1818 at Trier, of Jewish parents. In the revolutionary
year of 1848 he wrote the *Communist Manifesto* and returned from exile to
Cologne to edit the *Neue Rheinische Zeitung*

27 A sandstone carving of a Roman ship on the Moselle, carrying casks of wine and decorated with heads of wolves and gryphons. From the Stadtmuseum of Cologne

28 (*bottom*) A late Roman river god of the Rhine, also from Cologne

29 'The Watch on the Rhine', Spindler's setting of Audt's poem, which became a national war-song during the Franco-Prussian war of 1870

32   Sketches by Lyser of Beethoven, born in 1770 in Bonn, where he
lived until 1892. The remainder of his life was spent in Vienna

30   (*opposite above*) The re-occupation of the Rhineland by Hitler; German
troops at Ehrenbreitstein, near Coblenz, in 1936

31   (*opposite below*) Two architects of Franco-German friendship; General
de Gaulle and Chancellor Adenauer during the French President's visit
to Germany in 1963

35 (*top*) The thirteenth-century church of St Kunibert on the banks of the Rhine at Cologne with post-war buildings alongside. The church suffered damage during the last war, but has been restored

36 (*bottom*) The New Theatre at Cologne, one of the most striking buildings erected in the city since the war

33 (*opposite above*) Bomb damage in the old town at Bonn, which suffered severely during the last war. Today, the damage has been repaired, and many new buildings erected to accommodate the West German Government

34 (*opposite below*) The beautiful Romanesque Minster at Bonn, which in 1949 became the capital of the German Federal Republic

37 (*above*) A portrayal of the arrival of St Ursula at Cologne, with a view of the medieval city, by the Master of St Veronica

38 (*opposite below*) The Rhine at Cologne, showing the Cathedral, the Hohenzollern Bridge and the many modern buildings erected on the ruins created by air attack during the war

39 Refugees from air attack carrying their belongings across a temporary wooden bridge over the Rhine at Cologne; in the background are the ruins of the former stone bridge and the cathedral

40 (*above*) Schloss Augustus-
burg, at Brühl, near
Cologne, built by the
French architect Robert de
Cotte in 1782; the magnifi-
cent staircase is by Balthasar
Neumann

41   Carnival in Cologne,
which lasts for a period of
four months, culminating
in a spectacular procession
through the streets on the
eve of Good Friday

42 View of the industrial area around Duisberg, at the junction of the
Rhine and the Ruhr. It is the principal port for the iron and steel industry
of the Ruhr and itself an important centre of the metallurgical and chemical
industries

43 Goethe, born in 1749, in Frank-
furt-on-Main, where he spent his
childhood and youth. He later studied
at Strasbourg where he wrote *Gotz*,
Clanigo, *Wertber* and the original
draft of *Faust*

44 Heine, born in Düsseldorf in 1797.
The poet of German legend and ballad,
he was also one of the first and
greatest of modern journalists

45   Gold and enamel bust of the Emperor Charlemagne, from the Treasury
of the Cathedral at Aachen

46　Aerial landscape of the Lower Rhine

47   The docks at Rotterdam, now the largest and most modern port in the world. Rotterdam provides the main outlet to the sea of the river traffic of the Rhine

48 *Rotterdam*, by André Marquet, from the Musée de l'Art Moderne in Paris

49 The last waters of the Rhine: the river Maas at Rotterdam

the stale and somnolent atmosphere of its new capital is one of the striking paradoxes of the Federal Republic, as if a giant had chosen to live in some semi-detached villa, stuffy with the airs of the past and with aspidistra flying in the window.

On the banks of the Rhine an entirely new quarter has been built to accommodate the Parliament and the government and administration of the Federal Republic. But the most impressive of Bonn's new buildings, the Festival Hall, is dedicated not to politics but to the memory of one of the very greatest of the Rhineland's sons, Beethoven. Born in 1770, on his father's side he was of Flemish origin; his grandfather had been a singer and *Kapellmeister* at the electoral chapel and his father a tenor at the electoral court in Bonn. His mother came from a respectable family of the Rhine and Moselle area and before marrying his father had been the wife of a valet of the Elector of Trier.

Beethoven's father, who became a drunkard, so that after his mother's death Beethoven was appointed guardian to his two younger brothers, realized that in his son he had given birth to a musical prodigy. As early as 1782, at the age of twelve, Beethoven became deputy to the court organist, Christian Gotlob Neefe, who gave him his first regular musical instruction. At seventeen he set out for Vienna to meet Mozart, but was forced to return to Bonn by his mother's illness, which was followed a year later by her death. In 1792, he again went to Vienna, where he was sent by his patron, Count Waldstein, to study under Haydn. He never returned to Bonn or to the Rhineland.

Thus, like so many of the Rhineland's distinguished sons, Beethoven from an early age lived and died in exile from his native land. Yet in his case, as in theirs, the Rhineland left permanent marks upon him. His fierce love of independence, his democratic outlook, his resentment of the aristocracy, are all characteristics which many Rhinelanders have shared, without sharing his genius. Goethe, in his lofty way wrote, 'I am astonished by his genius, but unfortunately he is an altogether untamed personality.' In others like Georg Büchner, the same 'untamed personality' turned them into revolutionaries. A whole generation of Rhinelanders experienced the same revulsion of feeling which made him first dedicate his Third Symphony to Napoleon, whom he, like them, had welcomed as a liberator, and later destroy his dedication when Napoleon declared himself Emperor. And it has been suggested that his profound love of nature, which we hear at its clearest in his Pastoral Symphony, was first inspired by the beauty of the landscape around Bonn and the nearby Siebengebirge in which he was born.

A more vigorous rival to Cologne is Düsseldorf, lower down the river on the right bank. It was once the capital of the Duchy of Berg, after the Duchy had passed to the Electors Palatine; for a short period, after the destruction of Heidelberg and until the Electors transferred their residence to Mannheim, it became a flourishing centre of artistic and social life in the Rhineland. Its Academy of Fine Arts, a fine building in the Renaissance style founded by the Elector Charles Theodore in 1767 and restored after the last war, was re-established in 1819 and during the nineteenth century exercised a decisive influence on German painting. Reduced to rubble by air attack in the Second World War, Düsseldorf is today a newly built, modern, even elegant, city, a great river port, the capital of Nordrhein-Westfalen, and the financial and administrative centre of the Rhineland industrial area. If Cologne belongs very much to the past, Düsseldorf today belongs wholly to the present and the future.

Just as the spirit of the young Goethe hovers over Frankfurt, so that of the young Heine belongs to Düsseldorf. He was born there in 1797 and for several years of his youth, from 1807–13, lived under the French occupation. It is significant that Heine's memories of the occupation left him, like Goethe, not with feelings of hostility to the invader but with an abiding love of France; one day, in exile, he was to say that he lived in Paris 'like a fish in water', and certainly the French were always more sympathetic to him emotionally and intellectually than his Prussian fellow countrymen of whom he wrote so bitterly and sardonically. From Düsseldorf, the young Heine was sent to pursue a commercial apprenticeship in Frankfurt, and later in Hamburg; he returned to the Rhineland to study law in Bonn, and then left the Rhineland for ever, on the travels which took him first to Göttingen, where he studied under Schlegel, and later to Berlin, to England and finally to Paris, where he spent the last twenty years of his life.

Thus, like so many of his talented fellow countrymen, Heine spent the greater part of his life away from the Rhineland, yet in exile continued to bear the marks of his origin, in his cosmopolitanism, his love of France, his stubborn resistance to the Prussian spirit of authoritarianism and autocracy. There has never been a sharper, or a wittier, critic of reaction as it showed itself in Prussian form. In his lifelong polemic against the Germany which developed out of the defeat of Napoleon, he showed a profound insight into both the German character and German institutions. The poet of the Lorelei was also one of the first and greatest of modern journalists, with a gift of prophetic vision which made him more than a journalist; his travel sketches of the Rhineland in his *Reisebilder*, are among the best that have ever been written.

Before Düsseldorf became its capital, the centre of the Duchy of Berg lay east of the Rhine, in the basin of its tributary the Wupper, which together with the river Dhunn cuts a steep and tortuous valley through the hills on the northern edge of the Sauerland. The little town of Berg, with the castle of the Counts of Berg, stands on the banks of the Wupper as it makes a sharp turn from south to west before entering the Rhine; their original home had been at Altenberg, in the woods of the Dhunn valley, with its marvellous Cistercian abbey, which today serves as the Headquarters of the German Catholic Youth Association. No greater contrast could be found to these little towns, with their memorials of the past, sunk in their wooded valleys, than the industrial cities of Solingen and Remscheid, lying on both sides of the Wupper north of Berg, the first famous for centuries for the tempered steel, as fine as that of Damascus, of its sword blades and later the centre of the German cutlery trade, the German Sheffield. Here industrial development along the bottom of the valley, on both sides of the river, is continuous. Wuppertal, formed in 1929 by the union of Barmen, Elberfeld and neighbouring townships is a vast industrial conurbation extending for miles along the river, where today the traditional production of textiles is combined with newer industries like chemicals and engineering.

The textile industry of the Wuppertal gave his first experience of the harsh conditions of early capitalism to Friedrich Engels, Karl Marx's lifelong friend and patron, and collaborator in *The Communist Manifesto*, originally written as propaganda for a revolutionary organization, the *Bund der Kommunisten* (Communist League). He was born in Barmen in 1820, the son of a prosperous cotton manufacturer. Like Marx, he left Germany for England after the failure of the revolution of 1848, though in more comfortable circumstances. In Manchester, he became first an employee and later a partner in his father's textile firm, enjoyed the pleasures of an English country gentleman, maintained a working class Irish mistress, and continued his studies in scientific socialism.

The industrial area of the Wuppertal lies directly east of Düsseldorf, which serves as the river port for its products. North of the Wupper lies the even greater industrial concentration of the Ruhr, with Duisburg, the birthplace of Mercator, as its outlet in the river. From the junction of the Ruhr with the Rhine at Duisburg, a densely populated belt, nearly twenty miles broad and fifty miles long, extends continuously along the Ruhr, through Essen, the capital of the industrial empire of Fr. Krupp of Essen, the largest and most powerful industrial organization in the world which remains the personal possession of a single individual, and Dortmund, where beer rivals iron and steel as an industry. Fr. Krupp of Essen has had a world significance greater than any of the historical dynasties which have arisen in the Rhineland. The main base of the armaments industry which twice enabled Germany to conduct a war against a world in arms, confiscated by the allies at the end of the Second World War, and later returned to its present owner, Alfried Krupp von Bohlen und Halbach, it has today achieved even greater prosperity in production for entirely peaceful purposes. The history of the firm of Fr. Krupp of Essen provides one more example of the capacity for survival, and of continuity maintained through dramatic and sometimes disastrous changes which is one of the most striking characteristics of the Rhineland and its people.

Duisburg, on the banks of the Rhine immediately west of Essen, has by reason of its position at the junction of the Rhine and Ruhr become the greatest inland port in the world, surpassing even Mannheim; its docks extend for nearly twenty miles along the Rhine; they serve as a point of export along the river for the industrial products of the river and of import for the grain, foodstuffs and raw materials required to support its dense industrial population. Duisburg is also itself an important manufacturing city, with large steel and engineering works, and shipyards where most of the heavy barges and tugs are built for the Rhine traffic. The recovery of the Ruhr industrial area from the appalling destruction it suffered during the war, when some of its cities, like Dortmund or Essen, were virtually obliterated, is an achievement which is certainly very near a miracle and again an extraordinary demonstration of the vitality and capacity for endurance of the Germans of the Rhine basin.

Yet near this vast industrial concentration, one can still find on the banks of the river ancient little towns that seem to belong wholly to the past, and indeed it is this close conjunction of past and present, in the sharpest contrast with each other, which contributes much of its particular flavour to the life of the Rhineland. Zons, a few miles below Cologne, is the Sontium of the Romans, still encircled by its fourteenth-century walls and towers; in the fine Romanesque church at Kaiserswerth, north of Düsseldorf, lie the bones of yet another of the Irish monks who carried Christianity up the Rhine; English Protestant exiles of the reign of Bloody Mary found a place of worship in the Gothic church at Wesel, at the mouth of the Lippe. And the river's ancient and most legendary past is enshrined in the little town of Xanten, once the *Colonia Trajana* of the Romans and the birthplace of Siegfried, the hero who more than any other personifies the Rhine.

Xanten stands on the left bank of the river, below Wesel, with Rheinsberg and Moors to the south of it and Kalkar and Cleves to the north. All of these towns lie away from the river, at the foot

of the slope which overlooks its flood plain. All were founded at
a time when the river curved west away from its present course.
Cleves is built around a hill on which stands a tower, the
Schwanenturm, with a wide vista, north, south and east over the
flat plain and the river; to the west of it is a single hill, over three
hundred feet high, that stands out like a mountain from the
surrounding lowland, and beyond it is the forest of the Reichs-
wald. The chain of towns stretching south from Cleves along the
foot of the slope is completed by Krefeld, a manufacturing town
long famous for its textiles and now also a centre of the engineering and chemical industry.

To the west of the Rhine below Bonn, and parallel with it for
a distance of a hundred miles, runs a valley, beginning in the
Eifel, through which flows first the Erft, until its course turns east
to the Rhine, and then the sluggish stream of the Niers flowing
north to join the Meuse. On the left bank of the Niers stands the
great manufacturing town of München-Gladbach and below it,
almost on the Dutch frontier, the little towns of Gelders and
Goch. Another group of towns lies in the valley of the Roer,
rising in the Hohe Venn not far from the Belgian frontier and
flowing north-west to meet the Meuse, with Düren on its right
bank, half way between Cologne and Aachen, and below it,
north of the road from Aachen to Cologne, the little town of
Jülich, which was once the capital of the Duchy.

The centre of the area is Aachen, or Aix-la-Chapelle, on the
edge of the coalfield which here extends out of Belgium into
Germany and on the upper reaches of the river Wurm, a tributary
of the Roer. Aachen today is a manufacturing town of 170,000
inhabitants, gravely damaged in the last war, but splendidly restored and rebuilt, with magnificent parks and open spaces. It
was once the *Acquis Granum* or *Acquae Grani* of the Romans, who
were attracted there, as visitors still are today, by its hot springs,
and later the favourite residence of Charlemagne, whose love for
his 'Ais, le Capele' is celebrated in the *Chanson de Roland*. The
tomb of the great emperor lies in the cathedral, together with his
treasure and the holy relics which he collected there, still today an
objective of pilgrimage.

The Frankish kings also made Aachen their residence; to its hot springs it added the attraction of the hunting provided by the great forests in the neighbourhood. It was also of strategic importance because of its position on the road west from Cologne on the Rhine to the Meuse and Flanders and to northern France. To the south of the town are the hills which are the beginning of the plateau which stretches east to the Rhine gorge; once they lay on the border which divided the territories of the east and the west Franks, and it was natural that Charlemagne should have built his palace at this central point of the great empire in which the Teutonic and the Romance countries of Europe should be reconciled and united. The octagonal church which he built, the scene of the coronation of thirty emperors, still stands, built after Byzantine models with marble and granite taken from Rome and Ravenna; under the mosaics of the vault lies the great plain slab of black marble which is Charlemagne's tombstone, inscribed with two words only, yet sufficient to suggest all his magnificence; *Carolo Magno*.

West of Aachen, which is itself the most westerly of the historic cities of the Rhine basin, lies the point at which the Meuse, forming for a short distance the boundary between Belgium and the Netherlands, changes its name to the Maas. From its source on the edge of the plateau of Lorraine, it has flowed north parallel with the Rhine for a distance of 150 miles without receiving a single important tributary, crossed the western edge of the Ardennes by a steep and tortuous valley resembling the gorge of the Moselle, and at Namur emerged from their foothills to descend into the plain of the Netherlands. There it takes a right angled turn north-east, to follow the direction of its tributary the Sambre as far as Liège, where it gradually turns north and finally west to mingle its waters with those of the Rhine in the delta which forms their common outlet to the sea.

The northern edge of the Sambre-Meuse valley is continuous and unbroken by any tributary; from the brink of the valley a low tableland declines northwards into the Flemish lowlands around Brussels. Thus the valley cuts straight across Belgium, as the Ruhr does across Westphalia; the main sources of its water come from the south, the Meuse entering the valley at Namur, and the tributaries forming the Ourthe at Liège. From the table-land on its west bank, the drainage is not south into the valley but northwards away from it to the Scheldt.

The courses of the Scheldt and the Meuse follow a similar pattern. Both come from the south and receive their most important tributaries from the west, the Sambre joining the Meuse at Nancy and the Lys joining the Scheldt at Namur; then both rivers turn sharply east, following the direction of their tributaries, then north, the Meuse at Liège and the Scheldt at Antwerp, and finally west to the sea. The Scheldt, however, draining the low plateau north of the Sambre-Meuse valley is slow and sluggish, while the Meuse, fed by the waters of the Ardennes, is a fast flowing river.

East of Antwerp, between the Scheldt and the Meuse, lies an area of sterile sandy dunes, divided by the Dutch-Belgian border; west of Antwerp, where the surface soil is also naturally sandy, the work of centuries of intensive cultivation has mixed it with the clay beneath, so as to make Flanders one of the most fertile areas in Europe. But the most naturally fertile area of the Scheldt basin is the province of Hainault, through which the Scheldt flows from its southern sources in the foothills of the Ardennes past Cambrai, Valenciennes and Tournai.

In the division of Charlemagne's empire, the Scheldt appears to have been adopted as roughly the natural frontier between the western kingdom of Carolingia and the central kingdom of Lotharingia. In 887, the country east of the Scheldt, together with Lower Lotharingia, which included what is modern Belgium and the French department of the Nord from Dunkirk to Lille and extended east across the Rhine to Saxony, passed to Germany. When in the Middle Ages the Duchy of Lotharingia ceased to exist, its territory fell apart into a number of minor principalities. The County of Berg, east of the Rhine, and Cologne and Jülich west of it, were later reunited with Cleves and part of the Duchy of Flanders to form the Prussian Rhine province. Other portions of Lotharingia have been inherited by modern Belgium; the Duchy of Brabant, which includes the sandy hills of the Campine and the upper valley of the river Rupel; the County of Hainault, east of the Scheldt including the upper basin of the Sambre; the County of Namur, around the junction of the Sambre and the Meuse; the Bishopric of Liège in the Sambre-Meuse basin; the Duchy of Limburg, embracing the hills of the Vesdre between Liège and Aachen. The medieval organization of the territories of Lotharingia, in which Aachen and Cologne achieved indepen-dence as free cities, endured for centuries and insured that, with the exception of the basin of the Lys, they belonged politically as well as physically to the essentially German Rhineland. To the south, on the Rhine plateau, the Duchy of Luxembourg absorbed lands which had belonged partly to Upper and partly to Lower Lotharingia, dividing the basins of the upper Moselle and upper Meuse from that of the lower Meuse and the Scheldt.

In the later Middle Ages, the house of Burgundy, based on Brabant and with its capital at Brussels, gradually established its sovereignty over the western territories of Lower Lotharingia, with the exception of the ecclesiastical state of Liège; in Germany, the Dukes of Burgundy had Brabant, Limburg and Luxembourg, Namur and Hainault, and the lands of the Rhine delta to the north of them; in France, Flanders and Artois. Under Louis XIV the western borders of Flanders and Hainault and all of Artois returned to the French crown to become the modern depart-ments of the Nord and the Pas de Calais. For a few years, after the French revolution, Belgium and Germany west of the Rhine also became a part of France; in 1815, as the result of the secularization of Liège and Cologne, it was possible to organize these territories into the Prussian Rhine province, and the Belgian provinces of the Kingdom of the Netherlands; in 1830 Belgium and the Netherlands were divided, Belgium losing the south-eastern portion of Luxembourg.

The European importance of the Scheldt and the lower Meuse has depended both on strategic and on industrial factors. Strategically, the Scheldt and the Meuse divide Belgium into three parallel belts of territory. North of the Scheldt, between Ghent and Antwerp, the once marshy land is low-lying and liable to flood. South of the Meuse, the country is fissured by steep gorges and rises to the summit of the Ardennes. Between the two lies an open, dry, low-lying plain, fifty miles broad, which provides the easiest access westwards from the Lower Rhine into France. Within the plain, however, difficulties of terrain further constrict the approach route, so that the way west into France or east into Germany forms a narrow defile crossing the Meuse at Maastricht and passing by Brussels. The military problem is further complicated because this narrow front of advance is exposed to flank attack from England, so that it is scarred by battlefields which are drenched with English blood. This area is also the cradle of the race of Charlemagne; its founder, Pepin, Mayor of the Palace, was born at Neerwinden, west of the Meuse.

The passage through Lower Lotharingia was important commercially as well as strategically. At Cologne the Rhine traffic from Italy met the overland traffic from the Baltic and their merchandise was there unloaded for carriage west into Flanders. The prosperity of Ghent, Bruges and other cities of Flanders, originally founded on the native-grown flax which supplied their linen industry, and on the privileges extracted from their feudal overlords, financially crippled by crusading adventures, came to depend even more on the advantages they gained from their nearness to England, which supplied wool for the cloth industry, and from their easy communications, via Malines, Brussels, Louvain, Liège, Maastricht and Aachen, with Cologne and the great trade routes to which it was the gate by land and water.

In more recent times, however, the Flemish cities declined in commercial importance because of the growth of the great port of Antwerp, on the estuary of the Scheldt, and the development of the coalfield of the Sambre-Meuse valley and the upper Scheldt. As the great coalfield east of the Rhine follows the northern edge of the Westerwald, so the coalfield west of the river follows the edge of the Ardennes; their continuity is broken by the projection of the northern plain which extends past Cologne to Bonn. The western field begins near Aachen, just within Germany, follows the Sambre-Meuse valley through

Liège, Mons, and Charleroi, and near Mons and Valenciennes crosses into France between Douai and Lens, south of Lille. Between Liège and Valenciennes, however, there is a break in the coalbed, so that the coalfield falls into two parts, German and Belgian around Aachen and Liège, French and Belgian around Charleroi and Lille.

The industrial area around Charleroi, Mons and Valenciennes has the advantage of an elaborate and extensive system of waterways, which joins the Scheldt, Sambre, Somme and Oise basins by canals and canalized rivers and provides cheap bulk transport between Ghent and Antwerp, Paris, Namur and Liège, and up the Meuse to Mezières and Sedan. The rivers of Belgium, which belong essentially to the basin of the Rhine, have had as great an influence on the commercial and industrial development of the area as the strategic importance of the Meuse and Scheldt valleys has had on its political and military history.

THE DELTA

The Rhine leaves Germany, and ceases to be a German river, north-west of Cleves, and having crossed the Dutch frontier at Emmerich almost immediately divides into a number of channels in which its identity is lost. Just as, on its upper reaches in Switzerland, it collects the waters of innumerable streams, uniting them into a single great river, so after leaving Germany is discharges them through an intricate pattern of separate channels to the sea. If the Rhine has no single beginning, so also it has no single end.

Virgil describes the Rhine as 'two-horned', because of the two main channels into which it first divides, though in his day and up to the eighteenth century the division took place ten miles further up the river, within Germany and not Holland. Today the division takes place as the river turns west after leaving Germany. The left hand channel, the Waal, carries about two-thirds of the Rhine waters and the right hand, the Lek, about one third; each divides into a number of different channels and with the waters of the Waal mingle those of the Meuse on their way to the sea.

From the earlier part of the division within Germany, a dead channel runs north-west to join the right hand fork of the Rhine, the Lek, below Pannerden; below this junction the river takes the name of the Lower Rhine as it approaches Arnhem. Above Arnhem, it throws off a branch to the north, the Ijssel, which flows east and then north round the sands of Veluwe to enter the Zuider Zee halfway along its eastern bank, and continues through the shoals of the Zuider Zee, past Stavoren, to fork east and west before entering the North Sea. The Ijssel flows parallel to the Rhine from near Wesel; a similar stream follows the right bank of the Rhine from Cleves until it joins the Waal below Pannerden. The mouths of the Ijssel carry perhaps a tenth of the water of the Rhine.

From Arnhem, the Nieder or Lower Rhine flows west, with the sandhills of the island of Veluwe, the good island, on its right bank, and the meadows of Betuwe, the bad island, on its left. Beyond Veluwe it is protected by high dykes. At Wijk bij Duurstede, below which the river becomes the Lek, it throws off a narrow winding stream, the Kromme Rijn, or Crooked Rhine, controlled by lock gates as far as Utrecht, where it divides to flow north as the Vecht to the Zuider Zee, and west past Leyden as the Old Rhine. The Vecht again gives off a branch, the Amstel, which curves north-west through Amsterdam to join the river Ij, once a tributary of the Zuider Zee but now divided from it by a dam and connected directly with the ocean by the North Sea Canal. The Old Rhine also flows direct to the sea by a passage through the sand dunes to Katwijk; sea gates have been built to protect it against the North Sea tides, and when the gates are closed, the Old Rhine at Leyden is a dead river. It carries no more than a five hundredth part of the Rhine waters.

The greater part of these waters is carried by the left hand fork of the Rhine at the Dutch frontier, the Waal. Between it and the Lek lies the island of Betuwe, its meadows protected against flooding by high dykes. The left bank of the Waal, however, like the right bank of the Lower Rhine at Arnhem, rises to higher ground, a continuation of the ridge on which Cleves stands across the German frontier; at the end of the ridge is Nijmwegen, corresponding to Arnhem on the right bank of the Lower Rhine.

To the south of Nijmwegen lies the Meuse, now the Maas, whose course here turns from north to west and, beyond Nijmwegen, approaches the Waal so closely that the two rivers are only artificially prevented from joining. The Maas is diverted away from the Waal on a south-westerly course round the island of Bommelerwaard, and only finally joins the Waal fifty miles lower down at Gorinchem.

Of the two rivers the Maas is the smaller, carrying only a tenth of the volume of the water of the Rhine as it enters Holland, but it gives its name to several of the estuaries by which the waters of the Rhine enter the North Sea. Below Gorinchem the combined stream of the Maas and the Waal turns south-west and spreads out into a wide expanse of water like a lake, studded with islands and known as the Biesbosch or Reedwood. The clear channel through its shallow waters, the New Meerwede, emerges to form the wide estuary of the Hollandsch Diep, which broadens out as it turns to north-west into the ten-mile-long expanse of the Haringvliet; where it meets the sea the estuary has become so broad that the sand dunes on either bank are hardly visible across the water.

From the Waal, where it turns south-west to become the New Meerwede, another channel, the Meerwede proper, continues west to Dordrecht, on its left bank. Here the Meerwede divides; one channel flows north as the Noord to join the Lek and another continues west, as the Old Maas, along the south bank of the island of Ijsselmonde. Along the northern bank flow the joint waters of the Lek and the Noord, under the name of the New Maas, to Rotterdam, today the world's greatest port. The Old and the New Maas, combining the waters of the Rhine and the Meuse, join at the westernmost point of Ijsselmonde and, as the Brielle Maas, flow past the little town of Brielle to the sea; the burden of sea-going traffic, however, is carried by an artificial channel which has been driven to the sea at the Hook of Holland slightly north of the river's natural course. From the Old Maas, below Dordrecht, two navigable channels flow south to the

Hollandsche Diep and the Haringvliet. South of the Haringvliet, on a hill which stands out sharply from the sandy plain, stands Bergen op Zoom, at the head of the estuary of the East Scheldt, divided by the islands of Beveland and Walcheren from the estuary of the West Scheldt, which carries to the sea the bulk of the waters of the Scheldt.

The intricate pattern of the various branches of the Waal, the Lek and the Maas, in the broad alluvial plain of central Holland, forms the delta of the Rhine. No river's end could be more different from its beginning. The torrents that pour out of the Alps have been transformed into slow, sluggish meandering streams, all intricately interconnected, depositing on their way the silt which in the course of centuries has built up the rich alluvial soil of the Netherlands. In this sense, indeed, it might be said that Holland is literally a creation of the Rhine; Napoleon thought it rightly belonged to him because he had conquered Switzerland, where the Rhine has its source.

But today the deposits which the river carries down to the delta are by no means wholly a blessing. In the past the market gardeners and bulb growers of Holland have looked to the Rhine to supply a large part of their needs for fresh, non-saline water. By today, those waters on their course through the dense industrial areas which they traverse have been so heavily polluted that by the time the Rhine crosses the Dutch frontier at Emmerich it carries down forty thousand tons of salt a day as well as other industrial waste products.

This process of pollution began with the growth of industry on the banks of the Rhine in the nineteenth century, but it is only since the war that it has reached the stage which constitutes a serious danger to the states which adjoin the river, each of which has increasing and pressing demands for pure water both for domestic and industrial purposes. In 1880, the riparian states of the Rhine signed a convention to protect the salmon of the river; today, pollution has advanced so far that the river has no fish worth catching; only eels survive, which will survive anything. But eels caught in the Rhine today have to be kept for weeks in clear water to rid them of the taste of phenol.

The Rhine is still a great river, indeed commercially and industrially an even greater river than ever, but today it is also, alas, a dirty river. This is only one, if the latest, of the many changes which it has undergone during past centuries. Just as on its upper reaches in Switzerland there are dead valleys where the river once flowed, so it is likely that at its mouth the whole delta has in the past swung west for a distance of over sixty miles. But just as the Rhine has survived geographical and geological changes so it is likely that, with improved methods of waste control, and increasing international concern in the problem of pollution, the river will one day be saved from the damage inflicted on it by modern industry. In 1965, the newly constituted International Commission for the Protection of the Waters of the Rhine, representing the four riparian states and Luxembourg, began its work; it is a matter of encouragement for all those who love the Rhine that the economic and industrial needs of the states concerned must force them increasingly to restore and preserve the purity of its waters.

6 Legends

The facts of history and geography have both played their part
in the influence which the Rhine has had on the development of
Europe; but if we were to try to measure the hold which the
river has had on men's minds, we should have to enter another
world in which fact is inextricably combined with fiction, and
events, places, persons assume an extra dimension in myth and in
legend. No river has ever been quite so productive as the Rhine
of those tales of imagination and fancy in which peoples and
races have tried to express the hopes and fears with which they
invest the external world. In some of these the river itself is
personified, sometimes smiling and beneficent, sometimes cruel
and destructive; the stories with which it is associated seem to
take their colour and shape from its landscape, gay and bucolic
among sunny slopes and vineyards, gloomy and sombre where
dark forests press down to the river's edge and under forbidding
crags treacherous eddies lure the traveller to his doom.

In other stories, the river is personified in the many shapes and
forms in which flowing water may present itself to the imagination of a people, as sprites and nymphs, coiling serpents, marine
monsters, pixies and kelpies that sit on the river bank combing
their golden hair, while the woods and forests on the river's edge
are populated by gnomes and dwarfs who mine the hills for gold
and silver, or, like the Cooper of Auerbach, in subterranean
chambers brew wine more delicious than any mortal has tasted.
In mossy caves, saints and eremites dwell in solitude and silence,
until disturbed by a late traveller who turns out to be an Emperor
in disguise; in the forests wild huntsmen forever pursue the souls
of the damned; lovers leap across crags that have never been

bridged; from castle walls girls throw themselves in despair into the green and cruel waters that eddy beneath them.

All along the Rhine one may find these stories that give to each city, village and locality its appropriate ghost. There is hardly a place on the river bank that has not in some way or another been touched by the supernatural. Hundreds of these stories have been recorded. Taken together, they represent an immense treasure of folk memory, sometimes embroidered into the most sophisticated forms of courtly romance, in which elements derived from history, Celtic, Teutonic, classical, medieval and modern, from religion, pagan and Christian, from geography and topography, have all been woven together into a tapestry of which one can no longer distinguish the separate strands.

The church of St Ursula at Cologne commemorates a voyage which carried the saint from Britain to Rome. Attended by eleven thousand virgins, she sailed in splendour up the Rhine to Cologne, from thence to Basle and up the valley of the Rhône. In Rome she was received by Pope Cyriacus and with his blessing married Conan, son of the Roman Prince Agrippa. But in another form the Christian saint was also the Teutonic goddess Ursa or Hörsel, who at night sails across the skies in her silver boat attended by the innumerable train of her maidens, the stars. As the goddess of love, she entered into the Venusberg or Hörselburg in Thuringia, where she made Tannhauser captive to the charms of sex.

In such a story, history, religion, geography are all combined into a legend which, so far as ordinary men and women are concerned, has a more powerful and more permanent influence than the bare facts out of which it is composed, if they ever existed at all. Throughout the Rhineland one finds innumerable examples of the wonderful power of a race or a people to give to the objective world the shape of their own fears and desires. Knights, emperors, bishops, noblemen, whose objective existence is a matter of recorded history, make their appearance in legend endowed with supernatural powers and surrounded by the mysterious aura of people who move in a world that is outside common experience.

Sometimes a living legend is in such curious contrast with

recorded fact that we feel we are looking at history upside down or perhaps through the eyes of people whose ideas and feelings for the most part escape the notice of the historian. Thus Hatto, Archbishop of Mainz in the tenth century, was an able and energetic administrator under whom the city enjoyed great prosperity; but in legend he appears as a cruel and vicious ruler, an oppressor of the poor, who was abominated for his misdeeds; his dreadful end was once familiar to many English children in Southey's poetical version of the legend.

In a year of flood and pestilence, when summer and autumn had been so wet that the corn was still green in the winter, the Archbishop played a cruel and cynical trick on the starving peasants. He invited them to his well-stocked granary to provide themselves with the corn for the winter and when they had entered closed the doors on them and burnt it down. He was delighted with the lesson he had taught his serfs; but in the morning his frightened servants reported that during the night all the corn in his granaries had been devoured by a huge army of rats which was now advancing on his palace. The Archbishop fled to his tower on a rocky island in the Rhine near Bingen, which for centuries has been known as the Mouse Tower; but the rats pursued him, poured into the tower by windows and doors and through floors and ceilings and devoured the Archbishop until only his bare bones remained. Another story relates how the wicked Archbishop tricked and brought to his death the lord of the tower of Ehrenfels, which stands facing the Mouse Tower on the opposite bank of the Rhine.

But the greatest of the historical figures who appears in the legends of the Rhine is Charlemagne, and the number of stories attached to his name is evidence of how deeply his achievements stirred the imagination of the Germanic peoples. Once he was nearly brought to his death by the Rhine. At St Goar, at the foot of the Rheinfels in the Rhine gorge, as Charlemagne and his court were sailing up the Rhine, a sudden storm arose, so violent that his fleet was nearly wrecked. It was a sign of divine displeasure because the Emperor had failed to pay his respects to the shrine of the holy hermit of St Goar. The Emperor repented his omission, the storm subsided as suddenly as it had arisen and the river became as smooth as glass. The Emperor and his court put ashore where they spent the day in prayer at the shrine, presented the monastery with rich gifts and endowed it with large estates. It was at the shrine of St Goar also that Charlemagne's two sons, Pepin and Karloman, were reconciled as they sailed up the Rhine to attend the Imperial Diet at Thionville in 806 where their father proposed to partition his kingdom.

It is only natural that in these stories, in which the Rhine figures so largely, serpents and river monsters should play their part. At Zürich a great serpent appeared at Charlemagne's court and presented him with a magnificent diamond, set in a golden ring. It was not only of great beauty and immense value but had the magic quality that anyone who received it as a gift became the object of the giver's deepest affection. Charlemagne gave it to his fourth wife, Fastrada, and immediately became violently infatuated with her and remained so until her death. The ring then passed into the possession of Turpin, Archbishop of Rheims, and Charlemagne's affections passed with it, in such intensity indeed that they became an embarrassment to the Archbishop. He threw the ring into the moat surrounding the Emperor's palace at Aachen, and for the rest of his life Charlemagne remained passionately devoted to that city and it was there that he was buried.

The Rhine was also the scene of Charlemagne's wars against the Saxons, which are recounted in the fifth of the romances of the Twelve Peers of France, written by Jean Bodel in the thirteenth century. At Laon Charlemagne received the news that the Saxons had captured Cologne, defeated the Frankish forces and overrun the country. Charlemagne advanced to the Rhine at a point opposite the Saxon king's palace at Tremoigne, which reputedly is Dortmund. For two and a half years the Emperor was held up by the river, until at length a bridge was built, his army passed over, and Charlemagne killed the Saxon king in single combat. At one point in the war, Charlemagne escaped from an ambush laid for him by the Saxons, with the help of a deer who found him a way across the Rhine; at the point where he met the deer he founded the city of Frankfurt.

At Ingelheim, he was visited by an angel who gave him the strange command to go forth and rob his neighbour. Charlemagne at first resisted but then obeyed and was led into many strange adventures; but he successfully accomplished his mission and named the town, in which he held his court, the Angel's Home in memory of his heavenly visitor.

In the legends of Charlemagne the Rhine appears in its dual function as a frontier between hostile and warring nations and as a waterway which provides a passage from the north to the south of Charlemagne's dominions. But the most beautiful story of the Rhine as a waterway belongs to a later period than Charlemagne's. The original story of Lohengrin, the Knight of the Swan, comes from the *Chanson de Gestes*; the first German version appears in Wolfram von Eschenbach's thirteenth-century epic, *Parzival*. In this, the beautiful Elsa of Brabant has been incarcerated in the castle of Cleves by her guardian Frederick, appointed by her dead father. She has refused his hand in marriage and has been thrown into a dungeon to await her wedding day. An appeal is made on her behalf to the Emperor Henry 1; he pronounces that Elsa shall appoint a champion who will decide the question in single combat with her guardian. Elsa is unable to find a champion; she prays to the Virgin and in her despair beats her breast with her chaplet, from which hangs a little silver bell.

The little bell has magic properties. When its owner is in distress, its tiny silvery note swells in volume the further it travels; now it crosses the country until it peals like thunder above the temple where Parsifal and his knights guard the Holy Grail. To them it seems like a call for help from the holy vessel which they guard; while they are discussing what the message may mean, a mysterious voice is heard directing Parsifal to send his son Lohengrin to the rescue of Elsa. Lohengrin is to marry her, but must never reveal to her who he is.

Lohengrin obeys the command and sets out on his quest. On the banks of the Rhine he finds a boat drawn by a swan, in which he travels down the river; as he goes down the river, the air is filled with the most enchanting music. He arrives at Cleves on the day appointed for Elsa's wedding. He sees her face at the window of her prison cell, proclaims himself her champion, and defeats Frederick in single combat. Elsa invites him to claim his reward; he asks for her hand in marriage, adding that he can only stay with her so long as she never asks him to reveal his identity.

They marry, have children and enjoy great happiness. But Elsa is consumed by curiosity; she fancies that she is aggrieved, and her children humiliated, by having a husband and a father who has no name. She questions him; sorrowfully he reproaches her for breaking her promise, reveals who he is, and prepares to take his departure. She begs him to forgive her but it is too late; Lohengrin blows a long blast on his silver horn, the air is filled by the same music which announced his arrival, and on the river appears the swandrawn boat to carry him back up the Rhine to the temple of the Holy Grail.

The legend of the Knight of the Swan is common to many literatures and many stories, and probably has its original source in the ancient fairy story of the Seven Swans. After Wolfram von Eschenbach's version it was elaborated in many later ones, and it was from one of these later versions that Wagner took the libretto for his opera. But in no country perhaps has the story become so acclimatized as in Germany, and with no locality is it so closely associated as with the banks of the Rhine, and in modern times Wagner has made this association all the closer. In Wolfram von Eschenbach, the original sources of the story have been enriched by elements taken from Arthurian romance and Christian and courtly tradition; but much of its charm comes from the river itself and the water spirits which spring so naturally from it.

In other stories, these spirits seem to exist for their own sake, innocent of any later accretions, and it is significant that where this is so they nearly always carry with them associations of cruelty and destruction, as if it were the dangers and perils of the river that they are meant to symbolize. The most famous popular legend of the Rhine is that of the Lorelei, a maiden who lived on a steep and craggy rock which just out of the river near St Goar, and with siren songs lured travellers to their death. The name has been derived from Old High German *Lur*, to lurk, or lie in wait for, and *Lai*, a rock. In one version of the story an attempt is made to capture the Lorelei, who has led the son of the Prince Palatine to his death. A party of knights climbs the rock and cuts the Lorelei off from the landward side; in the moonlight, they stand transfixed at the sight of the nymph's long damp tresses, her shining eyes and smiling lips, and while they pause she summons up the waters of her father, the Rhine, which mount the cliffs in three great white-combed waves, drawing behind them a chariot which carries her into mid-stream where she sinks beneath the waters.

But in later and more popular versions, the cruel nymph is humanized and Christianized; as in the story of the Fair Maid of Bacharach, she becomes a lovelorn maiden whose lover has deserted her for the wars; by her beauty, coldness and indifference she drives all her other suitors to distraction and despair. Evil rumour ascribes her power to inspire love to her magic arts. She is seized and accused of witchcraft in the criminal court at Rhens, before the Archbishop of Cologne. She wins the heart of the Archbishop by her beauty, modesty and innocence and at her own request is allowed to seek peace in a convent across the river. A party of knights escorts her on her journey; as they pass the Lorelei she breaks away and climbs the rock to look for the last time at the castle of her false lover. But below her on the river she sees a boat, and her lover standing in its prow, returning from the war. She gives a wild cry so that his attention is distracted and the vessel is dashed to pieces on the rocks below; the maiden leaps from the cliff to die with her lover in the river.

Here all the original elements are transposed. Cruelty becomes beauty in distress; magic arts the calumnies of rumour, and the river receives the maiden, not as a father receives his daughter, but as the grave receives the injured and innocent. All that remains is that it is still the Lorelei which brings the sailor to his death.

In the Middle Ages, even the most hideous fantasies of popular imagination are subjected to the refining processes of civilization. Above Königswinter, on the right bank of the Rhine lies the Drachenfels, the Dragon's Rock, a dark mass of volcanic rock rising to one thousand feet and with a magnificent view across the river. Halfway up the rock is the Dragon's Cave which was once the home of a hideous water monster, half beast and half serpent, scaled like a fish and breathing fire from its nostrils. In pagan times it was the object of religious awe and veneration, and propitiated with human sacrifices.

Among its worshippers were two princes, who made frequent raids across the Rhine to secure captives who might be sacrificed to the monster. On one occasion they captured a Christian girl so beautiful that both princes fell in love with her and quarrelled for her possession. The priests of the Dragon sternly rebuked them and ordered that the girl should be offered up as a sacrifice. In the dawn, priests, princes, warriors and peasants marched in solemn procession to the Dragon's cave and there bound the girl to an legend. No river has ever been quite so productive as the Rhine oak which stood at its mouth. The monster emerged, dragging its heavy coils and breathing flame from mouth and nostrils. But the girl stood unafraid and as the beast fell upon her drew a crucifix from her bosom, so that the beast swerved aside in fear and plunged into the river. The power of the Cross, and the faith of its worshippers, led to the conversion of the pagans and their princes, one of whom married the girl and built for her a castle on the Drachenfels on the site of the ruins which still stand there today.

Yet the pagan deities driven out by Christianity sometimes tried vainly to return. Between Gernsbach and Eberstein was a chapel, the *Klingelkapelle*, the Tinkling Chapel. Once it was the shrine of the beautiful Teutonic goddess Herte, and when she was driven out became the moss-grown cell of a young hermit. One stormy night he gave shelter to a beautiful young girl who was lost in the forest. She revealed herself as the priestess of the goddess, the victim of cruel persecution by the Christians, and in the privacy of his cell practised all her arts of seduction on him to make him forget his vows. He was about to yield when above the noise of the storm he heard the tinkling of a bell which recalled him to his duty. The priestess vanished; outside his cell the hermit found a little silver bell hanging from a bough, and there he built the Tinkling Chapel.

Sometimes, however, it is the native spirits who are virtuous, and Christians and the Church itself, which are cruel, faithless and frivolous. Near the castle of Staufenberg was a clear and bubbling spring and there one day the lord of Staufenberg found a marvellous girl braiding her long, damp hair. She was a water nymph, and consented to marry him but only on condition that he always remained faithful to her. For years they lived in happiness together, and a little son was born to them, but at length the lord of Staufenberg was tempted away by the desire to win glory in the wars in France. There he won distinction in the army of a French prince who, to retain his services, offered him the hand of his daughter in marriage. The lord of Staufenberg had been seduced by the luxury and frivolity of the French court. He confessed to a priest that he was already married to a water nymph, and was relieved to be told that this was no Christian marriage but a union with an evil spirit. He married the Christian princess but at the wedding ceremony her hand was as cold as death, and as they crossed the bridge over a stream after leaving the church a violent storm arose, and the waters of the river flooded the bridge until they reached the knees of their horses. The knight recognized that the water nymph was punishing him for his broken oath and perished in the torrent. At the same moment a great storm raged round the castle of Staufenberg; the water nymph and her son disappeared, but ever after on a stormy night she could be heard weeping passionately while above the storm rose the wailing of a child.

Even the gnomes and dwarfs, the subterranean creatures who mined the gold and silver of the Rhine, may become figures of knightly romance, though not without retaining traces of their origin. In the forest of Zähringen lived a young charcoal burner, whose imagination had been fired by the impossible ambition of winning glory and honour in the tournament and the field. He confessed his dream to a hermit, who led him to a place in the forest where he was told he might make his fortune. There he found that the stone with which he built his kiln contained veins of pure gold, from which he amassed a great treasure. One night he gave shelter to a wanderer in the forest, starving and in rags; he revealed himself to be the Emperor, defeated in battle, and deserted and abandoned by his friends and vassals. The young man put his treasure at his service, with which the Emperor raised a new and victorious army; no one served in it with greater honour and distinction than the charcoal burner. He was knighted by the Emperor on the field of battle, and on the spot in the forest to which the hermit had led him he built a castle where the knights of Zähringen lived for ever after.

Yet for all the efforts made to exorcize the spirits of the wild that have inhabited the banks and waters of the Rhine, and to elevate them into a more refined world, in modern times it is precisely the element of the 'horrid', of the supernatural in the shape of evil, in the stories and legends of the Rhine which have given them their immense popularity. In this sense indeed the stories may be said to have made a very specific contribution to the sensibility of modern Europe, which is fundamentally a romantic sensibility, in which the supernatural and the irrational have played and continue to play a decisive part. It is on the Rhine that one can find the originals of those ruined castles and abbeys, the dungeons and torture chambers inhabited by depraved monks and evil spirits with which the eighteenth century liked to titillate a sophisticated taste; one can even find their shadows reflected, in a spirit of mockery, in Jane Austen's *Northanger Abbey*, which is a parody of the 'horrid' played out in the domestic elegance of Georgian England.

It would hardly be possible to understand the significance of the Gothic revival of the eighteenth century, and the romantic revolution in taste which followed, without in some way sharing in the sensibility to which the legends of the Rhine made such a powerful appeal. The stories were transmuted and adapted to suit the taste of a sophisticated age, often in ways that seem to us, as they seemed to Jane Austen, extravagantly silly; yet, even when corrupted by fashion, they sometimes have a genuine element of horror and morbidity in them, which is an essential part of romanticism, a sense that we live in an irrational world, in which the evidence of our senses, and the truths derived from them, may always be refuted by occult and secret forces with which we may, if we wish, enter into communication. When we speak of the scenery of the Rhine as romantic, we are not merely saying that it is beautiful, or dramatic, or deeply touched by history, though it is all of these; we mean that it has a particular quality which has helped to shape the sensibility of our age.

What was particular to the romantic sensibility was that it was one which took pleasure in the morbid, the cruel and the irrational. The Rhine stories are the product of a popular imagination for which both nature and society were filled with evil forces against which even religion was only a frail defence, but in their original form they have no suggestion that such a situation is capable of provoking pleasure, either in the participant or in the onlooker. No one can mistake, for instance, the genuine sense of revulsion, both religious and social, which underlies the many Rhineland stories of the Wild Huntsman who denies every instinct of religion and humanity in his passion for the chase.

In one of his many manifestations he appears as Hermann von Hernsberg, the lord of a castle on the Löwenburg. His love of the chase was so obsessive that he sacrificed to it every other interest, devastated the lands of his peasants and if they dared to protest set his hounds upon them and hunted them as human game; he was under the ban of the Church because he hunted both on the Lord's Day and on saints' days.

Once while out hunting he lost his way in the forest which surrounds the Löwenburg; tired by his efforts to find a way out, he lay down to sleep in an open glade. When he awoke, there emerged from a thicket a tall man of distinguished appearance, dressed in old-fashioned hunting clothes, a crossbow in his right hand, and a hunting horn and a knife hanging from his belt. He raised his horn to his lips and blew a terrible blast. In response, there appeared out of the forest hundreds of skeleton stags, each with a skeleton rider, who proceeded to hunt the stranger, driving him in a circle, the stags goring him with their antlers, the riders lashing him with their whips, until his body was torn and bleeding; but still the chase continued.

Von Hernsberg fainted with fear and horror. When he recovered his senses only the stranger remained. He told von Hernsberg that he was one of his ancestors and like him had been consumed by a passion for the chase. Once, in a period of famine his starving peasants broke into his preserves and carried off his game. In punishment, he had them seized and thrown into his dungeons where they were left to starve for three days. For the same period, his hounds were left without food, while his huntsmen caught the largest and strongest stags in the forest. Then the prisoners, or those of them who survived, were bound naked to the stags and the starving hounds set upon them, savaging man and beast, until by nightfall they killed the last of them in the clearing where the stranger now stood.

That night he died, and for ever was doomed to be hunted nightly from his castle court into the forest, suffering the torments both of the living and the damned, until the Last Day, when he would be hunted by legions of demons across the wastes of hell.

Such stories express, in a popular form, a kind of horror at the dark side of feudalism, and call in the supernatural to redress its wrongs; and this *motif* is one of the commonest in the legends of the Rhine. What gave the stories their immense popularity in the nineteenth century was precisely that this element of horror, and the gruesome details in which it was expressed, became a source of pleasure, of a kind of *frisson* which remains an essential element in modern literature and art. It was quite natural for Byron, in bidding farewell to the Rhine, to associate the 'Gothic' aspects of its scenery with the idea of a contented peasantry, as if for them also gloom provided the proper furnishing of happiness:

> The rolling stream, the precipice's gloom,
> The forest's growth, and Gothic walls between,
> The wild rocks shaped as they had turrets been,
> In mockery of men's art; and there withal
> A race of faces happy as the scene,
> Whose fertile bounties here extend to all
> Still springing o'er thy banks, though Empires
> near them fall.

But if dark forests, beetling cliffs, the river's treacherous whirlpools and eddies, and the spirits of the wild which inhabit them, provide the most appropriate setting for many of the legends of the Rhine, there is another group of stories which celebrate the goodness of life on the river, wine-bibbing, pleasure-loving and prosperous. It is significant that many of these come, not from the countryside, where the irrational is in the ascendant, but from the cities, in which men aim at the pleasures and freedoms of bourgeois life. For within the framework of feudalism, and threatening at times to break through it, the Rhineland cities enjoyed a period of great prosperity, of flourishing commerce and civic self-government, which, as Burckhardt points out in *The Civilization of the Renaissance in Italy*, provoked the envy of cities across the Alps, groaning under the despotism of a Frederick II or an Ezzelino da Romano.

Some of these stories directly reflect the conflict between feudal oppression, whether lay or ecclesiastical, and civic self-government; unlike the 'Gothic' tales of the countryside these usually have a happy ending. In 957 Cologne became a free city, under the nominal rule of its Archbishop, but with the right to administer its own affairs. But successive archbishops encroached on the city's privileges; ambitious and unscrupulous men, they tried to increase their own power by provoking dissension between the nobles and the citizens of Cologne. In the thirteenth century Archbishop Engelbert, not content with reducing the citizens' rights, tried to obtain control of the city's great treasure. He was opposed by the shrewd and able Burgomaster of Cologne, Hermann Grein, who succeeded in uniting the citizens and the nobles and restoring the city's privileges. The Archbishop determined to destroy Grein, and enlist in his plot two canons of a monastery near Cologne, which possessed a small menagerie, including a huge and savage lion. The Archbishop invited the Burgomaster to dine with him at the monastery to discuss the problems of the city. On his arrival, Grein was shown into a small high-walled courtyard, the gates were closed behind him, and he found himself face to face with the lion, which leaped savagely upon him. But Grein defended himself skilfully with his sword, and, though torn and mutilated, pierced the lion's heart with a swordthrust, before he fainted from loss of blood.

The citizens of Cologne became alarmed at Grein's long

absence in the monastery. The tocsin was sounded and the population hastened to his rescue. At the monastery they were told that the Burgomaster had strayed into the lion's den and been devoured. But they demanded to see his body and breaking down the gates of the courtyard they found the Burgomaster alive, though gravely wounded. They hanged the two canons at the entrance to the monastery, henceforward known as the Priests' Gate, and carried the Burgomaster back in triumph to Cologne.

In the stories and legends of the Rhine we can read what is a kind of folk version of the history of the river, though often so encrusted and embroidered by elements drawn from medieval romance and chivalry that its popular origin is obscured. The Middle Ages indeed are the richest source of the legends; but the hold which the river has exercised on the German peoples' imagination, of which the stories are a reflection, remained unbroken for centuries, and the stories themselves have helped to strengthen their feeling that the river is inalienably German. Bismarck was able to claim that in 1870 *Die Wacht am Rhein* had been worth three divisions to the German army; when the Reichstag on one occasion opposed an increase in Germany's armaments, and all efforts to persuade them had failed, he broke their resistance by a purely emotional appeal in which he quoted from the poem the lines;

> Es braust ein Ruf wie Donnerhall,
> Wie Schwertgeklirr und Wogenprall;
> Zum Rhein, zum Rhein, zum deutschen Rhein,
> Wer will des Strömes Hüter sein?
> Lieb Vaterland, magst ruhig sein,
> Fest steht und treu die Wacht am Rhein
>
> (There sounds a call like thunder
> Like clashing swords, like stormy waves.
> To the Rhine, the Rhine, the German Rhine!
> Who will this river's guardian be?
> Dear fatherland, have no fear;
> The watch on the Rhine stands fast and true.)

The deep emotional significance which the Rhine has had for the German people has its source among their most ancient memories; it is not fanciful to see in the modern wars which have raged on the Rhine a renewal and repetition of conflicts so old that only legend has preserved them. It is perhaps natural, therefore, that the river should have helped to inspire the greatest of all modern epic poems, the *Nibelungenlied*, which is indeed the greatest of all epic poems after the *Iliad*. And once again it seems an astonishing example of the river's continuing power to fertilize man's imagination that, in Wagner's hands, the *Nibelungenlied* should have provided the basis of what Thomas Mann has called the only true epic composed since the Renaissance.

In composing his opera, Wagner imported many elements into it that are not present in the original sources; but even in its earliest version, the story of the Nibelungenlied, its events and characters, seems specifically and surprisingly modern in a way that the *Iliad* for instance is not. Homer's men and women are divided from us by all the barriers that separate the pagan and classical world from our own; they have a serene nobility that is not possible in a civilization on which Christianity has cast its shadows. But the characters of the *Nibelungenlied* have the same divided natures as our own; even when heroes they are capable of crime; and indeed the poem is most easily understood as the history of a crime and its consequences. As the author of the latest translation of the poem into English says:

> The story which our poem tells is one of murder, and of revenge long nourished, and ends in the destruction of two armies. The avenger is a woman; the avenged her beloved husband; her victims are her brothers and kinsmen. This, in its crudest terms, is the plot.

We do not know the author of the poem; but it is probable that, as against the nineteenth-century view that it is the work of several hands, the poem only had one author, that he lived about 1200 AD, that he used material that had been the subject of heroic poetry for at least six hundred years, and was so successful in his treatment of it that all earlier versions of it have been forgotten and lost. But we know a great deal about the geography of the poem, of which the two poles are the Rhine in the west and the Danube in the east; the two rivers which in the medieval world provided the route between France and Constantinople. The story begins on the Rhine, in the historic city of Worms, the capital of the kingdom of the Burgundians, and at Xanten, from which Siegfried ruled a domain which included the Netherlands, Norway, and the land of the Nibelungs, and sailed down the river and over the sea to a mythical Iceland and its capital Isenstein. The first part of the poem centres on Siegfried and the Rhine; the second part on the Danube, and relates the doom and destruction of the Burgundians at the court of Etzel, or Attila, king of the Huns.

At the Burgundian Capital in Worms lived Kriemhild, the most beautiful woman in the world, under the guardianship of her three brothers, Gunther, Germot and Giselher. Down the Rhine, at Xanten, lived Siegfried, son of King Sigismund and his wife Sieglind, a young man who surpassed all others both in physical beauty and in feats of arms. He sails up the Rhine to Worms to seek the hand of Kriemhild, though warned that this may prove dangerous, and is there identified by Hagen, a vassal of King Gunther's, as the hero who has conquered the Nibelungs and become possessed of their fabulous treasure, has won from the dwarf Alberich his cloak of invisibility, and has killed a dragon and bathed in its blood, so that his skin has grown so horny that no human weapon can pierce it. Hagen fears the presence of so potent a hero at Gunther's court.

Siegfried lives at Worms for a year before he meets Kriemhild, but in the meanwhile wins her and Gunther's favour by leading the Burgundians victoriously against the invading Saxons. At the festivities held to celebrate the victory Siegfried is at last presented to Kriemhild, who emerges from her apartment like a dawn from dark clouds, and outshines all other women as the moon the stars.

The first act of the poem is accomplished in a mood which is the essence of romance; not a shadow passes across it, except for

Hagen's suspicions of Siegfried. The second act opens when the news is received at the Burgundian court that beyond the Rhine and over the sea there lives a queen of miraculous beauty and more than manly strength, whose hand can only be won by a man who can defeat her in three tests of physical skill. Her name is Brunhild and King Gunther determines to win her. He is advised by Hagen to take Siegfried with him on his wooing, especially, he hints, because of Siegfried's past relations with the lady; and Siegfried consents, on condition that in return for his assistance he shall be given Kriemhild's hand in marriage. To-gether Siegfried and Gunther, with their followers, sail down the Rhine and over the sea to Iceland. There Gunther wins Brunhild, but only because, in each of the three tests he has to pass, Gunther is aided by Siegfried in his cloak of invisibility. This is the first of many acts of deceit and treachery which punctuate the course of the poem.

Siegfried returns to Worms to prepare for the arrival of Gunther and Brunhild and to claim the hand of Kriemhild, which is willingly given. But the marriage of Brunhild and Gunther is unhappy; she is frigid to his lovemaking and on their bridal night resists and humiliates him. Once again Gunther calls on Siegfried, who impersonates Gunther in the darkness of the bridal chamber and in a violent struggle overpowers Brunhild and leaves her to Gunther, taking with him Brunhild's ring and silken girdle. Though the poem is politely reticent on the point, it is clear that in fact Siegfried rapes Brunhild in order to prepare her for Gunther. This is the second great act of deceit in the poem.

With his bride, Siegfried returns to his dominions at the mouth of the Rhine; when, at Brunhild's request, Gunther invites them on a visit to Worms, a violent quarrel breaks out between the two sisters-in-law, when Brunhild claims precedence over Kriemhild because, she says, Siegfried is a vassal of King Gunther's. Kriemhild replies by producing Brunhild's ring and girdle and asking, in the most insulting terms, how a Queen's lover can be her husband's vassal. This quarrel precipitates the tragedy which ends in the destruction of the Burgundians.

Hagen, as the faithful friend and servant of King Gunther,

takes Brunhild's part in the quarrel. He wins Kriemhild's confidence and discovers from her the flaw in Siegfried's invulnerability; when he bathed in the dragon's blood, a leaf had fallen between his shoulder blades, and at that spot a weapon can pierce his flesh. At a hunting party, Hagen lures Siegfried away into the forest and, while he is drinking at the spring, kills him by a spear thrust between the shoulders. After the murder of Siegfried, Kriemhild remains in Worms, though estranged from Gunther and Brunhild, and already meditating revenge. Hagen brings about a form of reconciliation, in order that the Burgundians may secure possession of the treasure of the Nibelungs; but when it is brought to Worms Kriemhild begins to distribute it to her friends and followers and Hagen, fearing the power she may acquire as a result, casts it into the Rhine.

This brings to an end the first part of the poem, in which the Rhine plays an essential part; indeed the mechanics of the story as we have it, would hardly be possible without the river. It is by the Rhine that Siegfried finds Kriemhild; it is the Rhine that carries Gunther to Brunhild and brings them both back to Worms; it is the Rhine that receives the fatal treasure of the Nibelung. And in Siegfried who has killed the dragon, and has bathed in its blood and thereby acquired his scaled and horny skin, we can recognize the true water-hero, who represents both the beauty and the power and the treacherous undercurrents of the river. And with his death, it is as if the Rhine itself had disappeared from the story.

Its second part is enacted on another great river, the Danube, where Etzel, king of the Huns has his court. A widower, he sends an embassy to Worms to ask for Kriemhild's hand, and she consents, seeing in marriage the means of achieving her revenge. Gunther also agrees, despite the warnings of Hagen, who throughout the poem shows the most profound psychological understanding of the motives of all the characters in the story. Indeed, one might say that the true hero of the *Nibelungenlied* is not Siegfried but Hagen, who never loses the sharp-witted and clear-sighted awareness of the mysterious danger which threatens his king and his people.

Kriemhild marries Etzel and after many years persuades him to invite Gunther to his court. Once again, Hagen is suspicious of Kriemhild's motives, but the Nibelungs, (with their treasure their name also has passed to the Burgundians) travelled from the Rhine to the Danube, moving from Worms towards the river Main and on the twelfth day striking the Danube somewhere near Mehring. This route in fact helps to date the events of the poem; at the time when it was written, a bridge had already been built across the Danube at Ravensburg and the natural route would have been Worms-Mietenberg-Würzburg-Nuremberg-Regensburg-Passau.

Once the Nibelungs are across the Danube, it becomes increasingly clear to them that Kriemhild's invitation has been a trap. They are massacred at a great banquet given in their honour by Etzel; Hagen, bound and helpless, is struck down by Kriemhild when he refuses to reveal where Siegfried's treasure lies buried beneath the waters of the Rhine, and Kriemhild herself is killed by an elderly knight in the retinue of the mythical Dietrich von Bern, the German King Arthur, who is a visitor at King Etzel's court. *Das ist de Nibelungnôt*; that is the story of the last stand of the Nibelungs, say the last words of the poem.

The *Nibelungenlied* is a great poetic masterpiece, and also in some respects a unique one. For though written in the classical period of medieval literature, in which the emphasis lay above all on the Christian and courtly virtues, and the refinement of taste which they encouraged, the *Nibelungenlied* is remarkable especially for its unrestrained violence of feeling, and its dominant theme of the lust for revenge untrammelled by any moral inhibitions. In these respects, it preserves the savage and pagan spirit of the Teutonic peoples in the age of the migrations. There appears to be little doubt that the origin of the story of the destruction of the Burgundians, or Nibelungs, is in fact to be found in the overthrow of the Burgundian kingdom on the Rhine by the Huns in 477 AD; while the strange, never wholly expressed or explained sexual relations between Siegfried and Brunhild, may reflect events in the dark history of the Merovingians.

Yet curiously enough it is precisely this more ancient and cruel tradition which gives the poem its strangely modern flavour. In the foreword to his new English translation of the poem, A. V. Hatto remarks that the poem can be read in precisely the same spirit as one reads a modern thriller, in which crime, revenge, violence, sadism, sex and the love of gold play their part. Yet despite the darkness of the story, the poem is illuminated by shafts of the purest romance; perhaps today what a traveller on the Rhine will most prefer to remember is the vision of Siegfried as he sails up the river, with his cloak of invisibility and the immense treasure he has conquered by his sword, towards the city where he and Kriemhild will meet in all the springtime of their beauty and their youth.

7 Art in the Rhineland

In the innumerable legends of the Rhine, we can see a picture of the river and its life as it has appeared in many ages in the strange, distorting, yet illuminating mirror of myth, folklore and romance. We can find an entirely different aspect of the river and of its history in the monuments of art and architecture which time has left on its banks, so many and so varied that even today, after all the ravages inflicted by time and human hands, they compose a marvellous gallery that shows us some of the most significant creations of European culture. They are the work of many generations and many races which have lived on the banks of the river; in creating them Romans, Christians, barbarians, Germans, Frenchmen, Dutchmen, Italians have all had a hand, and often it is the river itself which provided the means by which they came together and carried the materials with which they worked, like the stones of Cologne cathedral which were cut from the granite of the Rhine gorge. In this respect, as in so many others, the river discharged the essential function of a waterway uniting the lives of the many peoples, races and nations which have all contributed to the works of art which are to be found on its banks, like tributaries flowing into the river from infinitely distant and varied sources.

Of all these influences, none perhaps has been more significant or more enduring than that of the Romans who first brought civilization to the Rhine. Of what they built not much now remains, but everywhere along the Rhine, in the ruins left by the last war, evidence was found which showed how thoroughly they carried out their task of colonization and how deeply and widely their culture took root. A medieval copy of a Roman map preserved in Vienna shows the long chain of Roman towns which extended along the Rhine and its tributaries, with the road system by which they were connected and the baths, temples, public buildings and villas with which they were embellished. These Roman towns were the headquarters of the legions, and the remaining monuments that survive are often votive tablets and the headstones of soldiers' graves, sometimes crude and primitive, and dedicated to the religion of Mithras which the legions brought back with them from the east; they may be seen in the admirable collections of antiques in Bonn, Cologne, Wiesbaden, Karlsruhe, Mannheim, Speyer, Mainz and other cities of the Rhine. But at Trier especially, the most ancient of all German cities, with its rectangular town plan, its Porta Nigra, the three-storeyed city gate, towered for defence, the Aula Palatina, in turn palace market and hall of justice, its gigantic baths, its amphitheatre and bridge of Constantine, it is still possible to envisage what a city of the legions was actually like and to have a vivid sense of the life which filled its streets. And as an integral part of that life, one should include the colonies of Jews who followed in the path of the legions along the Rhine and left in their cities their own memorials of religion and culture.

In the towns on the left bank of the Rhine Roman civilization persisted up to the fifth and sixth centuries AD before it was finally submerged by the tidal wave of the Barbarian invasion. Yet in the ninth century it still had the power to inspire Charlemagne's dream of a new Roman Empire, in which not only Rome's political and military power but her arts and her literature should be restored and revived. No part of his empire benefited more from his piety, his love of learning and his munificence than the Rhineland and it was there, perhaps, that the new civilization he tried to create flourished most vigorously; the many legends of the great emperor that lingered for centuries along the Rhine are a kind of popular recognition of how much his peoples owed to him. Besides Charlemagne's palace at Aachen, his architect Eudes de Metz built a domed octagonal chapel, imitated from St Vitale at Ravenna, adorned with pillars of marble and granite, with wall paintings and mosaics and great doors and gates of bronze, which today forms part of the existing cathedral. The ground plan of the chapel served as a model for other churches along the Rhine, like Ottersheim in Alsace, and the pattern of its double row of columns was copied in the church of St Maria-im-Capitol at Cologne and in the Minster at Essen. It was built between 796 and 805, and at the same time Charlemagne's chancellor, Archbishop Hildebold, built his own cathedral at Cologne, a long basilica with a transept and apse at each end, of which the foundations have only recently been uncovered.

Nothing remains of Charlemagne's great palace at Ingelheim, the Angel's Home of the legend, which his chroniclers say was as splendid as that at Aachen; perhaps his most enduring memorial was the magnificent chain of abbeys, monasteries and churches, with their attendant libraries, academies of learning and art schools, which he founded throughout his empire, and not least on the Rhine. During the time of trouble which followed his death, they preserved and perpetuated the classical tradition of which they were the children. Out of them came the marvellous illustrated manuscripts of the schools of Aachen and Trier, with their stiff hieratic figures clothed in antique robes; at St Maximin at Trier, at St Pantaleon at Cologne, miniaturists, illuminators, workers in gold and enamel, in ivory and bronze, adapted to new purposes motifs derived from Rome and Byzantium. Sculptors and stone masons found inspiration in the same sources, as one can see in the capitals of the columns in the ninth-century church founded by Archbishop Otgar of Mainz at Höchst-am-Main, now an industrial suburb of Frankfurt, which show the direct influence of classical antiquity, yet are still wonderfully spontaneous and original.

Charlemagne's short, frail, unstable yet magnificent revival of the Roman empire was defeated by the renewed invasions of Germanic tribes from across the Rhine which followed his death, but even in such times of turmoil, distress and triumphant barbarism the long classical tradition continued to assert its vigour and vitality on the banks of the river. The eyes and minds of the Saxon and Franconian emperors of the eleventh and twelfth centuries were drawn irresistibly to Italy and to Rome by the prestige of their past glories, and they also enjoyed close and continuous relations with the new Rome of Byzantium; to the right of the high altar at St Pantaleon in Cologne is the tomb of the Greek princess Théophanou who married the emperor Otto II. On the banks of the Rhine especially, classical memories were kept alive by the wealth of examples that still survived of Roman and early Christian art, and the eyes and hands of workmen were familiar with classical architectural forms, which still enjoyed the glory that attached to their great past. In the towns, craftsmen were to be found who possessed a high degree of technical skill, and the river itself made it possible, when necessary, to import skilled labour from Italy and the south. In the frescoes which decorate the ninth-century church of St George at Oberzell, on the island of Reichenau below Lake Constance, in its miniatures and manuscripts and the green and gold and azure of their illuminations one can still see the work of an entire school of skilled artists and craftsmen which flourished in the great abbey.

The Carolingian tradition was equally preserved in the cathedral and abbey churches founded on the Rhine in the eleventh and twelfth centuries by the archbishops of Trier, Mainz and Cologne, with the support and assistance of the emperors. At Cologne, Speyer, Mainz, Worms, Trier, Strasbourg, Coblenz, Maria Laach, Andernach, Bonn, Schwarzrheindorf, such buildings reproduced until well into the thirteenth century, in plan, elevation and silhouette, the architectural forms which the Carolingians had adapted from antiquity, and together they form one of the most characteristic and most moving architectural features of the Rhine valley. Perhaps the most beautiful of all is the great Benedictine abbey church of St Maria Laach, on the wooded shores of the almost perfectly circular Laacher See in the Eifel, founded in 1093 and completed in 1156, with dome, transepts, two choirs and five towers, which still gives both in its general plan and in its detail a vivid impression of what a Carolingian cathedral was like; a certain plain and severe magnificence, a sense of mass and weight, an absence of decoration, for which the murals which decorated the interior were once a compensation and, more particularly on the Rhine, the highly individual outline of towers and spires silhouetted against the sky. In such a building, the architectural forms of the Romanesque are so deeply rooted that they seem to be a part of the landscape itself.

The remarkable continuity of artistic and architectural tradition was preserved along the Rhine until well into the thirteenth century; and it applied not only to the persistence of the Romanesque style long after Gothic had triumphed elsewhere, but to the very stones out of which the churches and abbeys of the Rhine were built. In the Middle Ages, Trier, Mainz, Cologne and other cities had a wealth of Roman remains, which builders and architects used as quarries from which they drew their material. Some of their most characteristic effects were obtained on the Rhine by using the light coloured Roman bricks to vary the stone facings of their round arches and by building in alternate bands of brick and stone; and when the supply of bricks began to give out, for the art of brickmaking had been lost, they obtained the same effect by using light and dark stone alternately. This use of alternate courses of varied coloured masonry is one of the most distinctive and pleasing features of the Romanesque churches of the Rhine.

As well as using the materials which the Romans had left behind, architects also used their foundations; as regards style, materials and site some of the Rhine churches might well be regarded as Roman buildings which have taken many centuries to complete. Thus the cathedral at Trier, which began as a Roman structure of the fourth century, was later converted into a Christian basilica and still later incorporated into the existing building. The church of St Gereon at Cologne, dedicated to the martyrs of the Theban legion and their captain Geron, victims of the persecution of the Christians under Diocletian, was originally a circular classical temple, said to have been erected by the empress Helena, which was converted into the existing octagonal nave in the thirteenth century. The technical methods of construction, up to the thirteenth century, were also classical, with the weight of the central dome carried on solid and massive walls, lightened by niches opening out into the interior, as in a classical rotunda.

The Romanesque churches of the Rhine are a singularly attractive feature of the river, in their gravity and simplicity, in their combination of classical and early Christian tradition, in a kind of serenity which is an effect of their use of space. In the twelfth and thirteenth centuries, the greatest centre of artistic activity on the river was Cologne, and many of their finest churches are the work of its builders and craftsmen, or were inspired by their example. Commerce had already made the city wealthy, and the growth of commerce stimulated a spirit of bourgeois enterprise and independence. Its clergy were both pious and learned and were also active and energetic administrators; religion itself was one of the sources of the city's wealth, owing to the fame of its holy relics, of the Theban legion, of St Ursula, martyred by the Huns, of the Three Magi, brought from Milan in 1164, which made Cologne one of the sacred places of Christendom, the rival as a place of pilgrimage to St Martin of Tours and St James of Compostella. Wealth, piety, political independence, commercial enterprise all combined to produce a great outburst of architectural activity. The old basilicas were rebuilt and great new projects were undertaken. In the eleventh century the magnificent church of St Maria-im-Capitol, on a site which according to legend was that of the Roman Capitol itself, had been built on a plan which, modified and adapted, became the model for a series of churches built at the end of the twelfth and the beginning of the thirteenth centuries: Gross St Martin, the Church of the Apostles, St Kunibert, with the choir and transept each terminated by an apse, giving the east end of the church a trefoil effect, and under the roof a gallery whose columns stood out against the dark background, producing the contrast of light and shade which was dear to the architects of the Rhine. To these beautiful churches of Cologne should be added others, at Xanten, Werden-an-der-Ruhr, Sinzig, Andernach, Germersheim, Bonn, which have added to the enormous wealth of Romanesque architecture to be found on the banks of the river.

The architects and craftsmen of this period added richness and variety to the Romanesque style by a variety of methods, by contrasting use of materials, by elaborating the detail and arrangement of arches and columns, by the use of sculptural decoration and mural paintings; the effect is one of richness and grandeur, very far removed from the simplicity and sobriety of early Romanesque, yet retaining its structural characteristics and demanding new powers of creativeness and invention. Little remains of the frescoes which decorated the interior walls, but at Bonn and at Schwarzrheindorf there is enough to show that the artists who executed them had considerable skill; in the decoration of both the interiors and the exteriors, in the carving of columns and capitals, the sculptors and craftsmen luxuriated in vegetable and mineral forms, dense foliage which encloses birds, serpents, humble beasts of burden, monsters—stone bestiaries which remind us that we are in the age in which the tales of Reynard the Fox were composed.

In part such developments may be attributed to close contacts with Italy and to the influence of Lombard artists who crossed the Alps by the Splügen or the Brenner and travelled by the valley of the Inn to Salzburg, Ratisbon, Passau, Augsburg and thence to north Germany, or by the Rhine to Alsace and the Rhineland, leaving marks of their passage behind them at Chur, Zürich, Basle, Speyer, Worms and Mainz. To the work of sculptors and masons, the Rhineland added that of the gold and silversmiths and brassfounders for which it had long been famous; from the workshops of Trier, of Cologne, of Aachen, came holy vessels and reliquaries of brilliantly enamelled gold; the reliquaries of St Heribert at Cologne-Deutz by Godefray de Huy, of the Three Magi in the cathedral at Cologne by Nicholas Verdun, are great masterpieces which show to what a degree of perfection the art of the goldsmith and the enameller had been brought on the Rhine. And in the reliquaries of the Virgin and of Charlemagne at Aachen we can see how that art was successfully adapting itself to the transition from Romanesque to Gothic.

For while the Romanesque was enjoying a late and splendid flowering which produced so many beautiful churches on the Rhine, an architectural revolution had already taken place in France, where Gothic had established itself completely and triumphantly. The influence of the new style, the inspiration of some of mankind's greatest artistic achievements, had reached the

Rhine by many channels, through the close relations which obtained between the emperors and the kings of France and between the French clergy and those of the Rhineland, and through the reports of German students who brought back the new doctrines from the schools at Laon, Chartres and Paris. By the beginning of the thirteenth century, the Cistercians had already built nearly fifty abbeys in Germany, which timidly at first, but later with more confidence, provided Gothic models for others to follow.

But the new style did not establish itself easily and especially in the Rhineland Romanesque continued to resist it. A stubborn struggle took place between innovators and traditionalists, which resulted in several buildings which are a curious hybrid between the two styles. The long persistence of the Romanesque along the Rhine illustrates how deeply rooted the classical tradition was, and how firmly attached its people were to the great memories of the past, even though the culture and the civilization to which they referred had been almost totally submerged under the tides of the barbarian invasion. And in this, it illustrates a more general characteristic which persists even today; a deep conservatism which, in spite of enormous political, social and industrial changes, still leaves the people of the Rhine valley profoundly tenacious of the forms of life and ways of thought of the past. Its most remarkable manifestation is, of course, the loyalty which they have shown to the Catholic religion, despite a bewildering sequence of political and social changes and the rapid and revolutionary industrial developments that have taken place on the banks of the river. This conservative religious and social outlook is perhaps all the more striking today, when it has survived both the shock of military defeat and the revolutionary technical and industrial changes induced by Germany's post-war economic revival, which are nowhere more evident than on the Rhine.

Loyalty to traditional forms could not be more strikingly displayed than in the long delay between the triumph of the Gothic style in France and its introduction into the valley of the Rhine. It was not until the beginning of the thirteenth century, when Gothic had already been fully established in France for

over fifty years, and had achieved some of its greatest masterpieces, that it made its first tentative appearance on the Rhine, in
Cologne, in the cathedrals of Mainz, Trier and Coblenz, and in
the beautiful Minster at Bonn. It can be seen in a more developed
form in the little chapel of the Templars built in 1200 at
Ramersdorf, above Königswinter, and in 1847 transferred to the
old cemetery in Bonn; or at Andernach, rebuilt in 1202, still in
the Romanesque style but with the influence of Gothic clearly
apparent in the pointed vaulting of the nave and the aisle.

Such innovations were almost certainly the work of French
architects, for Gothic was a French invention destined to revolu-
tionize architecture even on the Rhine, which resisted it longer
than anywhere else; a German chronicler referring to the Gothic
church of Wimpfen-im-Thal on the Neckar, begun in the
thirteenth century, described it simply as *opus francigenum*, a
French work. The beautiful cathedral of Limburg on the Lahn,
high on the cliffs overlooking the river, was the work of
architects and builders trained in the school of Laon, which,
with Soissons, deeply influenced the development of Gothic in
Germany in the thirteenth century. The Church of the Virgin at
Trier was copied from the church at Braine, near Soissons; the
cathedrals of Soissons and Tournai were copied as far afield as
Lübeck, Stralsund and Rostock. The sculptors of Rheims also
helped to bring Gothic to flower in Germany; their influence can
be followed at Bamberg, Magdeburg, Halberstadt and Naum-
burg, and, on the Rhine, at Freiburg and at Strasbourg.

In the early incursions of Gothic into the Rhineland, and elsewhere, the lower parts of the building remained, as before, heavy
and massive, but the vaulting and arcading of the upper portion
began to acquire the lightness and freedom of the new style;
often these features were superimposed on churches which
remained in other respects essentially Romanesque and sometimes, as in the nave at Freiburg, the difficulties which architects
found in reconciling the two styles are clearly apparent, even
though they are triumphantly overcome. Despite the transition
in styles, the cathedral at Freiburg, built entirely in dark red sandstone, is one of the most beautiful of all Rhineland churches.

The Gothic style did not entirely establish itself on the Rhine until the middle of the thirteenth century; there is thus a time lag of nearly a hundred years behind the development of Gothic in France. In the Church of the Virgin at Trier built between 1235 and 1260, the new style is completely triumphant. Together with Marburg, the church is in plan, elevation and decoration the first completely Gothic building in Germany; throughout French influence is dominant. That Trier should be one of the first places to surrender entirely to this influence was perhaps natural, because of the close relations that its clergy maintained with those of France, particularly in Rheims; French influence is equally apparent in Trier in the choir and vaulting of the cathedral and in the cloisters of the Church of St Mathias.

At St Mathias, however, Gothic is still at odds with Romanesque; the Church of the Virgin was intended and designed to be a purely Gothic building and a French architect, probably a native of Champagne, was called in who was familiar with the cathedral at Soissons and had worked at Rheims. The work of construction was assisted by the Archbishop of Cologne, the great builder, Conrad von Hofstedten, who in 1248 laid the foundation of his own Gothic cathedral of St Peter's. The French influence which is evident throughout the Church of the Virgin is strongest of all perhaps in the sculpture of the doorway, executed in the last third of the thirteenth century; here the marvellous skill of Chartres, Laon and Rheims have been completely transported to the Rhine, down to the last details of costume, gesture and attitude.

But the final step in the establishment of Gothic on the Rhine was taken with the dedication of the great cathedral at Cologne, which was to influence architecture throughout Germany. The old Romanesque cathedral was destroyed by fire on 30th April, 1248, and on the 15th August Conrad von Hofstedten laid the first stone of the choir of the new Gothic cathedral. It was planned on the model of Amiens and Beauvais, the latest and most spectacular of achievements of Gothic in France; what they had done for France, Cologne was to do for Germany. Its architect, Master Gerhard, is reputed to have been a native of Amiens; he was succeeded in 1280 by Master Arnold, and he in his turn by his son John in 1301. At first the building of the great edifice proceeded rapidly, but later it was repeatedly delayed by changes of plans and by lack of resources, and these difficulties are reflected in the many legends connected with the cathedral. For the size and grandeur of the new cathedral impressed themselves deeply on the popular imagination, as if it were to be the final crowning edifice of Christianity on the Rhine. But what was so hopefully begun, so superb an assertion of faith, was not to be completed until centuries later. The choir of the cathedral was dedicated by Archbishop Heinrich von Virnenburg in 1320, and the holy relics of the Three Magi solemnly displayed to the congregation. The choir was closed on the east by a temporary curtain wall, while work proceeded on the rest of the structure; the temporary wall was not removed until the nineteenth century and the cathedral itself was not finally completed, in one of the grandiose gestures of the new German empire, until 1880; among the nineteenth century additions are the cathedral's famous twin towers, one of the most striking architectural features of the city.

The long centuries during which the cathedral of Cologne came to completion have robbed it of the vitality and spontaneity of the great Gothic churches of the age of faith, and much of its structure today has the rigidity and uniformity of an archaeological reconstruction rather than a work of art. But in conception it was magnificent, and its twin towered façade, dominating the city from the little mound on which the cathedral is built, is one of the finest achievements of the German imagination. Elsewhere in the Rhineland Gothic achieved other triumphs. The cathedral at Metz was begun in the second half of the thirteenth century and its nave completed by the end of it. The cathedral at Strasbourg had begun in 1176, like its sister church at Freiburg, as a Romanesque building, one of the largest in Germany; Gothic had invaded the Rhineland while the apses and the transepts were still under construction, and the nave, begun in 1250, at almost the same date as the nave at Cologne, is almost completely in the new style. In 1277 work began on its beautiful façade, under the direction of Erwin von Steinbach, whom Goethe celebrated, and whose family remained in charge of the building operations until nearly a century later. Its octagonal tower, surmounted by a filigreed openwork spire is one of the most beautiful and original Gothic constructions in the Rhineland, though rivalled and perhaps even surpassed by the tower of Freiburg.

Cologne, Metz, Strasbourg, Freiburg and many other churches are triumphs of Gothic architecture in the Rhineland, where what was originally a purely French style achieved a new dimension under different conditions and in a different landscape; they are not works of imitation but have a vitality and originality of their own, as if they had sprung up naturally on the banks of the river and become completely assimilated and acclimatized there. They are indeed an essential part of the landscape of the Rhine; it would not occur to anyone that there was anything alien or imported in the spire of Strasbourg as seen from the Black Forest across the river. The same originality, the same air of intimately belonging to their surroundings, are to be found in the smaller churches built or rebuilt during the same period or later, at Altenberg and Xanten, in the beautiful church of St Catherine at Oppenheim, at Schleustadt and Weissenburg in Alsace, in the lovely late Gothic tower of St Theobald at Tann near Mulhouse.

The triumph of Gothic on the Rhine, apart from the structural changes it involved, also inspired Germans to emulate the French in the sculpture and statuary which were demanded for the decoration of Gothic churches. Unlike the Romanesque buildings of the Rhineland, with their plain surfaces covered with murals, the new Gothic cathedrals and churches offered every kind of opportunity to the sculptor. In the Gothic churches of the Rhineland, the carvings are sometimes beautiful, sometimes clumsy and grotesque; the best are to be found in the doorways of the Church of the Virgin at Trier and in the cathedrals of Strasbourg and Freiburg. One of the Rhineland's most magnificent examples of Gothic statuary, however, is not in stone but in bronze, the funeral effigy of the great builder and archbishop, Conrad von Hofstedten, which is in his own cathedral at Cologne.

The acclimatization of Gothic revolutionized church architecture on the Rhine; but questions of fashion and taste hardly affected the structure of the innumerable feudal strongholds whose ruins are such a distinctive feature of the landscape of the river and play so important a part in the appeal that it had for the romantic sensibility. For those castles which, overlooking the river amid its woods and crags, now charm the sentimental traveller, were built with a strictly utilitarian purpose of affording efficient means of defence and secure bases for attack, and since the art and technique of war changed very little until the end of the Middle Ages, the feudal castles of the Rhine retained the same fundamental structure for many centuries; war did not inspire the same stupendous flights of imagination as religion did in the ecclesiastical architects who built the great cathedrals. The interest of the Rhine castles, except for the very distinctive character they lend to the Rhine landscape, is literary and historical rather than aesthetic; the most interesting of them perhaps is the castle of the Katzenelnbogen at Reichenberg, near St Goarshausen in the Rhine gorge, with its tall crenellated towers and its spacious Herrenhaus, or residence, once of three storeys formed of three tiers of Romanesque columns which supported the high vaulted roof.

While Gothic was revolutionizing ecclesiastical architecture on the Rhine, painting was establishing itself as an independent art. Once restricted to the functions of providing frescoes for the bare interior walls of Romanesque churches, or the stained glass for their windows, painters now found new scope in producing altar pieces and easel paintings of the Holy Family and the saints for the embellishment of Gothic cathedrals and churches. In the development of painting, as of architecture, on the Rhine Cologne exercised a dominating influence and provided both the facilities and the inspiration for its first primitive school of independent masters. Inspired by the piety and the deeply mystical tendencies of catholicism in the holy city of the Rhineland they endowed their virgins and saints with a touching innocence and other-worldly charm, a freshness and awkward grace which adds yet another and highly distinctive image to the many which make up one's picture of the Rhine. For if we associate the river in some of its moods with the wild spirits of the waters and the woods, an equally truthful and significant reflection of it is to be found in the marvellous candour and sweetness of the St Veronica by some anonymous Cologne artist which is now in the Pinakothek at Munich.

The earliest known master of the Cologne school appears to have been Meister Wilhelm, who flourished at the end of the fourteenth century, though perhaps the only completely authentic work of his hands are the mural paintings from the Hanse-Saal of the Rathaus in Cologne; of the same school are the altarpiece of St. Clarissa in Cologne cathedral, and the *Madonna of the Sweet Peas* in the Cologne museum, dreaming, narrow-waisted girls who seem to be entirely absorbed in whatever thoughts of innocence and piety may occupy their minds.

These painters, known and unknown, were trying to paint the ideas which inspired the school of mystics which flourished in Cologne during the fourteenth century. The greatest of them, Meister Eckhardt, was born at Gotha in 1260, taught at Strasbourg and at Cologne from 1314 to his death in 1328. In 1326 he was charged with heresy; not surprisingly perhaps, for though he was the most popular preacher of his day in Germany, his doctrines owed as much to Aristotle, Plotinus the pseudo-Dionysus and Moses Maimonides as to Christian theologians like Augustine and St Thomas Aquinas.

Unum purum nihil; the one, the abstract, the nothing, was the conclusion he drew from his meditation on these masters, and he found many disciples to follow him, in particular Tauler, a native of Strasbourg, and St Nicholas of Suso, both pupils of Eckhardt's at Cologne. Suso's *Little Book of Truth* is still the most attractive literary expression of the school of mysticism which flourished in Cologne, but today it would have little meaning except to scholars if it were not for the narrow-waisted virgins of Cologne which make its doctrines real and palpable to us.

To the mysticism of the primitive masters of Cologne, Stefan Lochner, who came from near Constance and died in 1452, added a new sense of realism and a passionate interest in detail; the figures and faces of his virgins remained gentle, childish and immature, but their draperies, their jewellery, all the objects by which they are surrounded belong to the world of sense and not of spirit and are painted with a fidelity of one who loved the profane as much as, or even more than, the sacred. His greatest work is the triptych which he originally painted for the city hall in Cologne and which was removed to the chapel of St Michael in the cathedral in 1810, celebrating with a loving realism the saints and martyrs whose relics Cologne was so proud to possess; the Three Magi, St Gereon and his companions of the Theban legion, St Ursula and her eleven thousand virgins. Lochner's *Dombild* is a wonderful masterpiece; Dürer, on his travels in the Low Countries, noted in his diary that he had paid two silver pennies to see the great work by Meister Steffen in Cologne. But in the *Madonna of the Violets*, in the Archiepiscopal Museum, and the *Madonna of the Rose Arbour*, in the Cologne museum, one can see the same kind of poetic realism, which is akin to that of the Flemish primitive.

It is probable that Lochner was influenced by the painters who worked at the court of Burgundy in the fifteenth century. Their influence extended equally to the Upper Rhine and affected such painters as Martin Schöngauer of Colmar, Mathias Grünewald, and Hans Baldur Grien; by the end of the fifteenth century painting in the Rhineland was almost entirely under Flemish influence. Schöngauer, a pupil of Roger van der Weyden, was a great engraver even more than a painter; the best known of his work is the *Madonna of the Rose Garden* in the church of St Martin at Colmar. Grünewald, born at Würzburg in 1460, and court painter to the Archbishop of Mainz, carried naturalism to the point of cruelty, yet illuminated it in unearthly light and colour. A great painter, certainly one of the greatest of his day, his masterpiece was the six-winged altarpiece, depicting the youth and passion of Christ and the temptation of St Anthony, painted for the monastery church of St Anthony at Isenheim. In Hans Baldur Grien, of Strasbourg, who died in 1488, one can find equally a meticulous realism, combined with an obsession with the morbid and the extravagant, which one may be excused for thinking particularly characteristic of the Germanic imagination. In these fifteenth-century painters of the Upper Rhine, there is a marked originality of outlook, in which a scientific interest goes with an almost excessive power of feeling and fancy, which gives them a very special place in the history of European painting.

They might indeed be described, despite their dependence on Flemish models, as almost the last native and spontaneous flowering of the artistic impulse in the Rhineland, for in what followed them foreign influences became so strong and so dominant as almost to crush the independence of feeling that gives its particular interest to the medieval art of the Rhine. In the Middle Ages, the architects and artists of the Rhineland adapted both Romanesque and Gothic to their own purposes in such a way that both styles took deep roots on the banks of the river and became an integral part of the life of its people; they were popular arts in a sense in which art was never popular again. The façade or the silhouette of a Romanesque or Gothic church on the Rhine is never quite the same as it is elsewhere, even when they have been built in direct imitation of foreign models, and the difference reflects a different form of the imagination, a different attitude to life, a different social and economic environment.

In this sense, the Renaissance never became acclimatized or took deep root on the Rhine as Romanesque or Gothic had done. Partly this was due to a genuine decline in the vitality and originality of the creative impulse on the banks of the river and this went together with, and was partly a reflection of, a decline in its commercial prosperity and importance. The sixteenth century saw the beginning of the decline of the great free cities of the Rhine, whose wealth and influence passed to the Netherlands, while the ecclesiastical princes consolidated and strengthened their temporal power. Moreover, Europe had passed into an age when political power, and the culture that went with it, was expressed through the nation-state; in such an age the Rhineland had little to say.

When the Renaissance came to the Rhine, it came from Holland and France; the Italian Renaissance had strangely little influence.

For a time it met with some resistance in which the profoundly conservative and religious spirit of the region showed itself once again. Devoutly catholic the Rhineland remained faithful to the architectural ideas of the age of the great cathedrals; the Jesuits in particular exercised a conservative influence and continued to construct their churches on the Gothic model, with baroque decoration. Before Renaissance architecture conquered the Rhine, it had to survive a conflict with Gothic which produced a number of buildings in which both styles are curiously, and awkwardly, mixed.

Nevertheless, when the Renaissance style was once accepted, its victory was quickly complete, and even though it never took root as Gothic had done, from the middle of the sixteenth century onwards German architects, for the most part taking France as their model, produced a number of impressive Renaissance buildings on the banks of the Rhine. The grandest of these was the Schloss at Heidelberg; on the east side of its great courtyard is the Otto-Heinrichs-Bau, begun in 1596, with its splendid Italianate façade, the most beautiful of all German renaissance buildings; on the north side is the Friedrichs-Bau built between 1601 and 1607 by Johannes Schoch of Strasbourg, to designs in which Gothic features were still retained. The vast palace of the electoral princes of Mainz at Aschaffenburg was built between 1605 and 1616 by Riedinger in imitation of the chateau of Ancy-le-Franc; at Trier, the electoral palace was reconstructed after 1620 for the Archbishop Lothar von Metternich and today, with its beautiful eighteenth-century gardens, forms a wonderful architectural group with the Romanesque basilica which adjoins it. And the air attacks of the last war fortunately spared the beautiful early renaissance façade of the City Hall in Cologne, built in 1569 from the designs of Wilhelm Vernickel and decorated with reliefs which depict, alongside biblical heroes like Samson and Daniel, Burgomaster Grein and his fight with the lion.

These Renaissance works, together with the numerous châteaux and country houses in the Renaissance style which are to be found on the Upper Rhine, in the Palatinate and in Baden, were for the most part carried out by German architects, though dominated by French or Flemish influences. For a short period at the beginning of the eighteenth century, German architects working under Italian influence again produced some magnificent works of art in the Rhineland. Between 1719 and 1744 the great architect Jean Balthasar Naumann built for the Prince Archbishop of Würzburg the magnificent palace at Brüchsal, near Heidelberg, which was for a time the residence of the Archbishop of Speyer; perhaps the finest baroque building in the whole of Germany, it was one of the greatest architectural losses of the last war, but Naumann's work is also to be found in numerous churches along the Rhine, at Neresheim, Schönthal, Schwarzach, and in the church of St Paulin at Trier. His pupil Seitz was responsible for the two charming rococo pavilions which were added to the archiepiscopal palace at Trier. Catholicism also made Italian influence felt in the great monasteries built by the Premonstratensians and the Benedictines.

But art in the Rhineland in the eighteenth century was predominantly, after 1730 one might say exclusively, French art; it became the private possession of prince and courts who took not only their taste and their culture, but their architects from France. When in the next century Georg Büchner, himself a Rhinelander, in his *Hessische Landbote* proclaimed the slogan of *Friede dem Hütten; Krieg den Palästen* (Peace to the hovels; War on the palaces) he was not only making a political gesture; he was also protesting against the process by which art in the Rhineland had become wholly alienated from the soil and from the people.

In the eighteenth century, each petty prince, lay and ecclesiastical, in the Rhineland aspired to have his own version of Versailles, as lavish as his means could afford, and at Strasbourg, Trier, Mannheim, Mainz, Coblenz, Bonn and elsewhere imported French architects to satisfy their ambitions and their pretensions. The triumph of French art, of French culture, of French manners was as complete on the Rhine as the triumph of Gothic had ever been; but it was a triumph which was restricted to the princes and their courts. The political and cultural power and prestige of France were at their height and the petty principalities of the Rhineland had no native resources with which to resist them. The treaties of Westphalia had made Alsace a French province and Strasbourg a French city, while the electoral princes of the Rhine had become satellites and pensioners of the French crown. French culture and the French language became a social necessity for any Rhinelander with pretensions to rank or education, and a period of residence at the French court obligatory.

The prestige and charm of French cultural achievements inspired the rulers of the Rhineland with the ambition to reproduce them at their own courts and in their own style of living. As Louis xiv had abandoned Paris, so the princes of the Rhineland moved out of Cologne, Mainz, Trier and other capitals to build themselves French châteaux in the neighbourhood, designed by French architects and by French decorators, filled with French pictures and French furniture. A French writer has rightly said:

> The Rhine of the legends is crowded with splendid and charming monuments of the French art of the eighteenth century, and on its banks Robert de Cotte, Bouffrand, Jacques Francois Blondel, Peyre and their pupils have planted replicas of Versailles, Marly and Trianon.

A typical example of the domination of French taste was the palace, and neighbouring country house, built by the elector of Cologne at Bonn. In exile at Versailles from 1701 to 1714, he there conceived the desire to rebuild his palace in accordance with French taste and drew up plans for its reconstruction in conjunction with Robert de Cotte. On his return to his principality, the plans were put into effect, the work being supervised by Robert de Cotte from Paris. The palace, which is now the university, has been severely damaged by fire and drastically restored; but the country residence of Poppelsdorf nearby, with its beautiful gardens and magnificent avenue of chestnuts, its paintings and decorations entirely carried out by French hands, is a perfect example of French art transplanted to the banks of the Rhine. Robert de Cotte also drew up the plans for the beautiful Schloss Augustusburg, at Brühl, between Bonn and Cologne.

The building work was carried out by French architects, the decoration by French designers, the gardens were planted by a pupil of Le Nôtre; its magnificent staircase, however, is the work of Balthasar Naumann.

At Mainz, at Trier, at Mannheim, at Düsseldorf, at Karlsruhe and elsewhere French art established itself on the banks of the Rhine and added yet another beauty to its landscape. Much has been destroyed by war and by time, but in what remains the Rhine still has to offer an immense wealth of examples of the elegance and distinction of French eighteenth-century art.

With the nineteenth century, and the absorption of the Rhineland, first by Prussia and then by the new German Empire, the art of the Rhineland as such may be said to have come to an end. But the long cultural tradition of the Rhineland cities and their immense treasury of artistic remains continued to make them centres of intellectual and creative activity and made Cologne especially a powerful influence on the artistic life of Germany. In this century also the city has been distinguished by the eager welcome it gave to new movements in art and literature, to the French Impressionists and Post-Impressionists, to the artists of *Der Brücke* and *Der Blaue Reiter*, to Dada and Surrealism, and this responsiveness to what was new and creative has made its Wallraf-Richartz Museum one of the finest collections of modern art and sculpture in Europe.

But in the Rhineland, as in the rest of Germany, the willingness and eagerness to accept new ideas which was characteristic of the Weimar Republic came to an end with the victory of National Socialism, while the devastation caused by the war threatened to destroy all the material foundations of civilized life. In one sense indeed the destruction was so great that it presented Germany's architects and builders with an unparalleled opportunity for reconstructing and rebuilding all her cities, but unfortunately conditions were such that it was impossible to exploit this opportunity fully. The British Control Commission in the Rhineland regarded as wholly chimerical Dr Adenauer's plans for building an entirely new city of Cologne, at a time when millions were without a roof over their heads or any other form of shelter. The urgency and the immense scale of the purely material task to be achieved left little room for artistic considerations. Equally, National Socialism had driven into exile the brilliant generation of architects which between the wars had created the Bauhaus, first in Weimar and later in Dresden and had founded one of the great creative movements in modern architecture. It was not until 1960 that the greatest of them, Mies van der Rohe, was again commissioned to design a new building in Germany, an office block for Fr. Krupp of Essen.

The rebuilding of the Rhineland's ruined cities is an immensely impressive achievement, and the broad central avenue of a city like Düsseldorf now gives a hard and glittering effect of elegance and affluence. But it is precisely the shining glass-steel-concrete newness of the buildings that take the eye, especially when, as often, they lie side by side with Romanesque or Gothic structures that have endured for centuries. But many of the new buildings, especially of the vast numbers of new dwellings that have had to be built, are depressingly repetitive, mechanical and uninspired; there has been no attempt to emulate the experiments in working class housing that were carried out in Weimar Germany or in Vienna between the wars, and large areas have been rebuilt with little or no consideration for town planning. Indeed, it is only in recent years that the growing traffic congestion in the cities of the Rhineland has forced them into bold and spectacular measures to free themselves from the stranglehold of the traffic problem.

Nevertheless, among the vast mass of new construction in the Rhineland there are many admirable new buildings, some of them by younger architects who have emerged out of the ice-age imposed by National Socialism. Industry, for reasons of prestige and public relations, has contributed some of the best of them, like the Phoenix-Ruhrort skyscraper, by Helmut Hentrich and Herbert Petschnigg, or Mannesman's new office block, by Schneider-Esleben, both in Düsseldorf. Both the new Nord bridge at Düsseldorf and the Severin bridge at Cologne are bold and imaginative conceptions, the latter admirably successful in its placing in relation to the adjacent towers of the great cathedral. Many of the innumerable new churches that have been built are of a remarkably high architectural standard, especially in the archdiocese of Cologne, where, as elsewhere in Germany, the Catholic church has been among the leaders in architectural innovation; particularly remarkable are those of Rudolf Schwarz, with his aim of creating 'high inhabitable pictures like life-sized parables'. His church of Fronleichnam at Aachen and of St Michael at Frankfurt are both admirable successors to the magnificent tradition of ecclesiastical architecture on the Rhine. Music and the theatre have also provided architectural inspiration. Wolske's vast festival hall in Bonn, the Beethovenhalle, and the opera house in Cologne are both spectacular buildings which are among the finest of their kind in Europe. Lastly, in thinking of the cities of the Rhine today, one should not forget the immense and loving labour and care which have been devoted to restoring the damage inflicted by the war on their historic buildings, so that even today they constitute an inexhaustible treasury of the riches which have been left to the Rhine by the past.

8 War and Peace

The works of art which are to be found in such variety and splendour on the banks of the Rhine, are only one effect, though a glorious and enduring one, of the river's function as a meeting place for the cultures of many lands, races and peoples. One might find an equally significant example in the commercial history of the river, which has also depended on its function as a waterway uniting the north and the south of Europe, the North Sea with the Mediterranean, the basin of the Seine with the basin of the Danube. In the past, this aspect of the river has seemed to some people so much its most important one that they have believed the destiny of the Rhine valley was to provide a kind of proving ground on which some federalist organization of the state could be worked out which would be a model for the whole of Europe.

For such a view it would be easy to find support in the history and in the geography of the Rhine basin and in the character and temperament of its peoples, which for centuries has been moulded by the intimate contact with their neighbours which the river itself has encouraged. They have made of them people who were not easily assimilated into the rigid forms of the secular, centralized nation state which have dominated European politics for over two hundred years. Arndt, looking out across the river from his pedestal at Bonn, may have been right in proclaiming the Rhine a German river, not a German frontier, *Deutchland's Strom nicht Deutchland's Grenzr*, but this is not a view which the people of the Rhine valley have easily or willingly accepted. For centuries they looked west rather than east for their culture and their political ideas, displayed a remarkable freedom from the prejudices of race or language, and tried, though unsuccessfully,

to preserve their local forms of government against the encroach-
ments of the unified national state. In part, these attitudes were
the result of their deep attachment to the Catholic faith, which
made them profoundly conservative in the sense of clinging to
the supra-national institutions of the Catholic church, and
sceptical of the absolute, and revolutionary, claims to loyalty both
of nineteenth-century Prussia and of nineteenth-century France.

In these attitudes they preserved, perhaps longer than any other
people, the inheritance of the empire of Charlemagne; only at the
source and at the mouth of the river did they throw off this inheritance, or burden, from the past. Charlemagne's empire gave
birth to two institutions, for centuries intimately interconnected,
which both profoundly influenced the development of the Rhine
territories. The first was the Holy Roman Empire, which was the
heir of Charlemagne's attempt to unite Europe and revive the
glories of Rome; the second was the French monarchy, which
succeeded to his western kingdom. During the thousand years
which followed the dissolution of Charlemagne's empire both
these institutions were to suffer profound transformations; both
were to come to an end within a few years of each other, the
French monarchy in 1793, the Empire when it was suppressed by
Napoleon in 1806. In the interval, they had experienced very
different destinies. The French monarchy, before it fell, was to
grow into the most powerful of all European states, the creation
of 'the thirty kings who made France', until by the end of the
seventeenth century it surpassed all others in splendour and glory.
The Holy Roman Empire, as a political power, was to dwindle
until it was rather less than the shadow of a shadow. Yet both
these institutions, so different in their destinies, were to have a
profound influence on the development of the Rhine territories
and, in their relations with each other, continued for centuries to
have a direct effect on their political affairs.

The French monarchy, for its part, consciously preserved the
memory of its Carolingian origins, and of its historical connection
with the Rhine valley which had been the central axis of the
Carolingian empire. This inheritance was part of the divinity, the
charisma, the mysterious aura of supernatural grace and authority,

which surrounded the French throne; it found a curious reflection
in the custom by which every king of France, as late as Louis XVI,
sent the funeral pall of his predecessor to Aachen so that it might
lie on the tomb of the emperor. Such a custom was more than
purely empty form; it was a symbolic assertion of the claim that
Charlemagne had been the founder and protector of the French
monarchy and that the kingdom of France continued to be
intimately concerned with the Rhine territories which were the
centre of his empire.

The Holy Roman Empire, on the other hand, while its claims
to universal sovereignty became increasingly hollow, for centuries
still retained a certain political reality on the Rhine, both in its
power over men's minds and in its influence on their practical
affairs. For the Empire itself was very largely a Rhineland institu-
tion. Of the eight electoral princes of the Empire, four came from
the Rhine; the Elector Palatine was vicar of the Empire for the
Rhineland, Franconia, Swabia and Bavaria; the Archbishop of
Mainz presided over the imperial diet. Moreover, the three
ecclesiastical electors of the Rhine were not merely powerful
figures in the political intrigues which surrounded the election of
the Emperor; they were also temperal powers in virtue of the
authority that came down to them from Charlemagne, who had
governed as much through his bishops as his lay vassals, and both
their temporal and their ecclesiastical power extended to both
banks of the Rhine. The ecclesiastical province of Trier, whose
archbishop carried the title of Archchancellor of the Gauls,
extended across the river north of Mainz up the valley of the
Lahn. The authority of the Archbishop of Mainz, who was
primate of Germany, Archchancellor of the Empire, president of
the imperial diet, and who crowned the Emperor, stretched across
Germany east of the Rhine from Switzerland to Hamburg and
included Magdeburg, Augsburg and Bamberg; the province of
Cologne extended from the Meuse to the Wesel and included the
whole of Westphalia.

Thus political conditions on the Rhine came to.form a curious
intricate pattern, in which it was often difficult to distinguish
between the shadow and the reality. For as France assumed the

status of the greatest of European powers, the reality increasingly became its ambition to extend its power to the Rhine, and in the attempt to realize this ambition the ecclesiastical princes of the Rhine, their spiritual and temporal powers, their influence on both banks of the river and in the affairs of the Empire, their intimate relations with the French court and the French clergy, were all factors which had to be reckoned with. The affairs of the Empire and of the Rhine states became a matter of permanent and compelling interest of the French monarchy. The Treaty of Westphalia expressly stipulated that the king of France should sit in the imperial diet as Landgrave of Alsace. The ecclesiastical princes of the Rhine became paid pensioners of the king of France and active agents of French policy and French culture. By the end of the eighteenth century, all three of the ecclesiastical princes were relatives of Louis xvi. Clement Wenzel of Saxony, Archbishop of Trier, was his mother's brother. The Archduke Max Franz of Austria, Archbishop of Cologne, was the brother of the Emperor and of Marie Antoinette. At Trier, Mainz and Cologne the French monarchy maintained diplomatic missions which promoted French policy and made propaganda for the Gallican doctrines of the French Church in opposition to the Papacy; among their ranks were statesmen like Vergennes who pursued a policy based on Sully's ideas of a Christian Republic led by France, based not on conquest but peaceful penetration, the reign of justice and the autonomy of its member states.

French anxieties with regard to the Rhine increased with the rise of the House of Brandenburg, in which France came to see a greater danger than her hereditary enemy, the Hapsburgs. And indeed it was Prussia which finally put an end to French hopes of establishing on the Rhine a ring of independent states, a *boulevard de Paris* too weak to resist French influence but strong enough with her support to prevent the crossings of the Rhine from falling into the hands of an invader from the east. But French policy in the eighteenth century was effective and persuasive enough to leave the states of the Rhine with memories of a past in which, although German by race and language, they were not exclusively German and could combine a local independence and authority with the closest political and cultural realtions with their great neighbour to the west.

Such feelings, which were deliberately encouraged by France in the eighteenth century, as they were to be once again after 1918, were all the more natural on the Rhine because they coincided both with religious sentiment, which drew its people to Catholic France rather than Protestant Prussia, and with memories of the freedom and self-government which the Rhine cities had enjoyed in the Middle Ages. The Confederation of Free Cities founded by Mainz and Worms in 1254 had for a time included over a hundred towns, stretching from Basle and Zürich in the south to Cologne and Bremen in the north, and had been strong enough to compel the archbishops of Mainz, Trier and Cologne and the bishops of Worms, Strasbourg, Metz and Basle to join it. And if this form of political association also proved in the long run a failure, it nevertheless left on the Rhine a tradition of municipal autonomy and self-government which added yet another element which has made the people of the Rhine less amenable than their fellow Germans to the rigid structure of a modern centralized state.

The traditions of the empire of Charlemagne and the Holy Roman Empire; French influence, French culture and French prestige; the tradition of municipal autonomy inherited from the free cities of the Rhine; the temporal power of the ecclesiastical princes, extending to both banks of the Rhine; profound attachment to the Catholic faith; all these in combination were to give the people of the Rhine an outlook and a character which are markedly different from those of their fellow Germans to the east. Yet such influences, however strong they were in the past, and remain even today, were too weak to resist the explosive and revolutionary forces which, gathering strength throughout the eighteenth century, at its close shattered the traditional framework of Europe to west and east of the Rhine, to the west in the shape of the French revolution and to the east in that of the national German uprising provoked by the defeat of Prussia. No two movements could have been less alike in their ostensible ideals and aspirations. In the west, the armies of the revolution advanced to the Rhine under the banners of the rights of man and the principles of liberty, equality and fraternity. In the east, Prussia carried out its own revolution, and reconstructed herself, by demanding unconditional and selfless obedience to the state, and the sacrifice of the individual in the service of the nation conceived as a mystical community united by the ties of race, blood and language. But both were alike in appealing to the profound and revolutionary feeling of nationalism which henceforward were to dominate political developments in Europe.

Both movements were essentially hostile to the traditions and political attitudes which had taken such deep root along the Rhine, and in the protracted and violent struggle which broke out between revolutionary France and first Prussia, and later united Germany, the historic position of the Rhine territories as a weak, loosely organized association of states which provided both a buffer and a link between east and west was destroyed for ever; in the course of the struggle, the French provinces of Alsace and Lorraine were to change hands four times in seventy-five years, in 1870, in 1918, in 1940 and again in 1945 and the Rhine came to be regarded primarily, not as a great waterway providing a means of communications between nations, but as a frontier to be fought for until both France and Germany were defeated and exhausted.

Yet it is significant of feelings in the Rhineland that the armies of revolutionary France were at first welcomed, just as the French emigrés had at first been welcome at the courts of the ecclesiastical princes. Goethe, observing their arrival, wrote of it in similar terms to Stendhal's description of the French invasion of Italy; 'In appearance they brought nothing except friendship, and in fact friendship was what they offered; their souls were exalted; they light-heartedly planted gay trees of liberty. They promised everyone their own rights and their own government.' Speyer, Worms, Mainz and Frankfurt were occupied, and in March 1873 Mainz was annexed to France, only to be evacuated three months later. In September the French entered Aachen, which they occupied for twenty years, then Trier, Bonn, Coblenz, Düsseldorf and Mannheim; the left bank of the Rhine had been secured and the Revolution had completed the policy of the French monarchy.

Yet popular feeling turned against the French when it became
evident that what they intended was a policy of annexation;
Goethe, who observed this change of feeling, said that the French
'oppressed their neighbours whom they had called brothers'. To
pacify discontent, the Convention sent Lazare Hoche as a commissioner to administer 'the territories between the Meuse and
the Rhine and between the Rhine and the Moselle'. Hoche
carried out his task in the liberal spirit of Vergennes, suppressing
the administrative organs set up by the French and re-establishing
the local judiciary and the local administration, under the super-
vision of a commission composed of five French members; the
university of Bonn was reopened and the clergy permitted to
discharge their spiritual functions. His policy provoked hopes of
the establishment of a Rhineland republic which would be a
guarantee of peace between France and Germany; it found a
passionate supporter in the great Rhineland patriot, Görres.

When Hoche died prematurely at Wetzlar in 1797, he was
universally regretted; with the *coup d'état* of Fructidor of that
year, the French Directory reverted to a policy of annexation,
which was combined, under Napoleon, with a rigid policy of
centralization. In 1798, the French commissioner Rudlier made a
clean sweep of the past and divided the Rhineland into four
French departments which became an integral part of the French
state; the Roer, capital Aachen, and including Cologne, Crefeld
and Cleves; Rhine-and-Moselle, capital Coblenz, and including
Bonn; Mont-Tonnerre, capital Mannheim, including Speyer,
Mainz and Zweibrüken; the Saar, capital Trier, and including
Prüm, Saarbruken and Birkenfeld. This drastic territorial reorganization, which ignored all the traditions, aspirations and
administrative divisions of the Rhineland was inspired entirely by
French interests and administrative convenience. It transformed
the warm feelings for France which had subsisted in the
Rhineland into hostility and converted many of those who, like
Görres, had greeted the French as liberators into German patriots.
Moreover, the annexation of the Rhineland had to be paid for by
concessions to the east of the river, and Prussia received in compensation the secularized archbishoprics of Münster and

Paderborn, the principality of Hildesheim, and the abbeys of Elten, Essen and Werden; in all, 112 petty states were suppressed and divided among the German princes who had suffered a loss of territory on the left bank of the Rhine. In 1806, the Holy Roman Empire ceased to exist, after a thousand years of continuous existence. It was not the death of a political power, but of a political ideal.

The Napoleonic settlement on the Rhine gave France what the French monarchy had never achieved; the restoration of the ancient 'natural' frontier of Gaul. And even though the Napoleonic policy of annexation and administrative centralization affronted local patriotism and turned men's minds and hearts towards Prussia, French rule was sweetened, and in retrospect inspired grateful memories, because of the liberal and humane policies pursued by some of the French prefects of the new departments; Jean-Bon St André in the Mont-Tonnerre, Alexandre de Lameth, in the Roer, Adrien de Lézay-Marnésia in the Rhine-and-Moselle. Indeed, the tradition of friendship for France continued to survive in the Rhineland, even though it was not strong enough to resist the growing power of Prussia and the attractions of German patriotism and German national unity. Pro-French feeling was largely a reflection of the difficulty with which the Rhine territories adapted themselves to the framework of the new Germany created by Prussia in the image of Prussia. Catholic where Prussia was Protestant, German speaking, yet traditionally orientated towards France, with a deep sense of local patriotism and politically inclined towards federalism rather than rigid centralization, drawn by the river itself into close communication with lands far beyond their own boundaries, the peoples of the Rhine valley fitted awkwardly and reluctantly into the new Germany which developed in the nineteenth century and were temperamentally and emotionally ill at ease in it.

Napoleon's solution of the problem of the Rhine, though for a moment it gave France the illusion of security conferred by its ancient frontier, in the long run only weakened her position on the river. In the Europe created by the Congress of Vienna in 1815, Prussia received compensation for the loss of her Polish territories by a large addition of strength both on the right and on the left bank of the river, receiving the whole of Westphalia, and the Rhineland on both sides of the river from the Moselle to the Dutch frontier, and on the left bank also the area between the Moselle and the Nahe. These territories included the territories of Gelderland, Cleves, Jülich and Berg, the ecclesiastical states of Trier and Cologne, the free cities of Cologne and Aachen, and the lands of nearly a hundred small lordships and abbeys. They were first formed into the two Prussian provinces of Cleve-Burg and Lower Rhine and later, in 1824, consolidated into the Rhine Province.

Prussia thus became a state that stretched from east to west across the whole of Germany and beyond the Rhine, and thenceforward, as Prussia's, and Germany's, economic and military power increased, the problem of the Rhine was a constant source of anxiety to France until it became a kind of national neurosis that affected not only statesmen and politicians but men of letters and the ordinary man in the street. Alsace indeed remained in French hands, but she had lost that protective barrier, the *boulevard de Paris*, which guarded the crossings of the Rhine that exposed her to the perpetual threat of invasion from the east.

In this sense, the settlement of Vienna decisively altered the balance of power in Europe to the disadvantage of France and gave to the Rhine and the Rhine valley north of Alsace a strategic importance which it had not possessed since the days of the Romans. But in the period which has passed since the Congress of Vienna the strategic situation on the Rhine has in one crucial respect been the reverse of what it was when the river formed the frontier of the Roman Empire. The Romans had realized that though the Rhine might form a natural boundary for their Empire, it was not sufficient only to hold the left bank of the river. Security demanded the possession of a bridgehead on the right bank which would give control of the Rhine crossings both at their eastern and at their western ends. Thus the actual frontier, or *Limes*, of their Empire was an artificial one, which ran east of the river from its source to north of Cologne and gave them control not only of the river itself but of the approaches to its crossings. The settlement of Vienna reversed this position; it not only left Germany in possession of the whole of the right bank of the river, within the limits of her frontiers, but in the Rhine Province gave her a powerful bridgehead on the left bank of the river commanding the easiest and shortest routes into the heart of France. It was the possession of this bridgehead across the Rhine which made it possible for Germany to launch, with such paralyzing effect, the three violent assaults on the west which she delivered within a period of seventy years.

The violent nationalist feelings which broke out in France and Germany during the diplomatic crisis of 1840, inspiring Becker and Musset to their bellicose poetic claims to the Rhine, were a sign of how potent a symbol the river had become to the peoples of both countries; though even then there were some, like Victor Hugo, who hoped that French influence might be restored on the Rhine not as a result of war but of a restoration of amicable relations between France and Germany. And indeed pro-French feelings on the Rhine remained sufficiently strong to make such hopes not entirely unrealistic. When the abortive revolution of 1848 broke out in Germany, there were riots in Mannheim, Heidelberg and Mainz, and the *Marseillaise* was sung in the streets of Cologne; the Palatinate and Baden rose in revolt against Prussian domination of Germany and in support of a united Germany founded on the principles of liberty and democracy. Karl Marx, in the *Rheinische Zeitung*, called for the destruction of the relics of feudalism on the Rhine and for a revolution which would carry out in the Rhineland the same task that the French had accomplished in their own country in 1789. To such revolutionary manifestations Bismarck in the German Diet at Frankfurt returned the appropriate reply of the Junker; 'The people of Prussia have no intention of allowing its monarchy to founder in the corrupt manifestation of licence that has taken place in South Germany.'

Yet it is significant that by this time France as well as Germany had accepted the absolute validity of the principle of nationality which destroyed the basis of any form of autonomy on the banks of the Rhine. In 1848, France refused to lend any support to the risings in the Rhineland, in the Palatinate and in Baden, and when later, in preparation for his war against Austria, Bismarck tempted Napoleon III with the prospect of acquiring the area between the left bank of the Rhine and the Moselle, the French emperor considered that his own commitment to the principle of nationality compelled him to refuse; French policy remained limited to the hope that the states of the Rhine might retain sufficient independence to constitute a restraint on the aggressive policies of Prussia.

Such hopes were vain; what proved to be correct were French fears for her security as a result of the position secured by Prussia on the banks of the Rhine, and the Franco-Prussian war of 1870 proved how well-founded those fears were, not only politically, but militarily. In that war, the German plan of mobilization, designed to inflict a rapid and crushing defeat on the French, provided for the strategic development of the German army on the left bank of the river. The general staff calculated that the French would require four days to concentrate their forces around Strasbourg and Metz, with the bulk of them around Metz, and six days for them to march from Metz to the Rhine. The Prussian general staff therefore counted on a period of fourteen days to complete the deployment of their forces west of the river before the French could offer any serious opposition. Moreover, the delay imposed on the French by their approach march to the Rhine meant that the Germans could postpone a decision on the final detraining areas of their troops until after the French had revealed their intentions. Such a timetable, which was vital to the success of the German plan of campaign, was only made possible by their command of the crossings of the Rhine and the road and rail routes leading from them on the left bank of the river. The strategic advantage held by Germany made French defeat almost inevitable, unless redeemed by a superiority in men, material and organization which the French were far from possessing.

The crushing victory achieved by the Prussians was crowned by the annexation of Alsace and Lorraine. Thus the position which Napoleon had won for France on the Rhine was for forty-eight years, from 1870 to 1918, totally reversed to the advantage of

Germany. The entire left bank of the Rhine from Basle to the Dutch frontier was now in German hands; so great a strategic advantage might well have seemed irreversible. Yet, by one of the ironies of history, the annexation of Alsace-Lorraine proved to be one of the factors which made the position inherently unstable, creating in France so determined a national will to recover the lost provinces that any reconciliation between France and Germany became impossible.

Moreover, the German seizure of Alsace-Lorraine emphasized once again how unwillingly the people of the Rhine valley adapted themselves to the principle of nationality, interpreted exclusively in terms of race and language. Bismarck appears to have hoped initially that the German-speaking majority of the region would be easily and willingly assimilated into the new German empire. In fact, the population enthusiastically supported the French Republic which had been born out of military disaster and sent a delegation to the French National Assembly to protest against annexation to Germany. In 1874, the first parliamentary delegation representing Alsace-Lorraine in the German Reichstag repeated the protest.

Alsace-Lorraine had to be governed as a conquered province. In the new German empire it had the anomalous position of a *Reichsland*, a Reich territory which belonged neither to Prussia nor to any of the individual states of the empire but formed a province of the Reich as a whole. From 1879 to 1902 it was governed by a personal representative of the German Chancellor, with the now sinister name of *Reichstatthalter*, exercising the powers of the Chancellor, which included the power of declaring martial law. There could not have been a clearer confession of the difficulty of adapting Alsace-Lorraine to the constitutional structure of the German empire.

Yet though the population stubbornly refused to accept their new status as Germans, political developments in France also moderated their enthusiasm for the Third Republic. At the turn of the century, after the Dreyfus case, the French Republic adopted an increasingly anti-clerical policy; in Alsace-Lorraine, the clerical party which represented a majority of the population, and approved the compromise with the Catholic Church which Germany achieved at the end of Bismarck's *Kulturkampf*, came to favour an autonomous status within the framework of the Reich. Yet relations with the Reich government deteriorated as, after the fall of Bismarck, its policy became increasingly aggressive and pan-German; conflicts between the civil population and the large military garrison culminated in the riots at Zabern in 1913, when a German lieutenant insulted Alsatian recruits. To meet the growing hostility of the population, the German government even considered partitioning Alsace-Lorraine among the South German states, but under the pressure of war abandoned the project in favour of permitting a larger degree of autonomy.

The period of nearly fifty years in which Alsace-Lorraine formed part of Germany emphasized once again factors which have had a permanent influence on the political affairs of the German Rhine valley. The attraction exercised by France; the political importance of Catholic religious feeling and Catholic tradition; the powerful impulse towards local autonomy, either within France or within Germany; the relative weakness of language, race or nationality in determining political loyalty; the underlying hostility to government from Berlin; all these are influences to which the people of the Rhine valley have in greater or less degree been susceptible. They could be summarized as an instinctive antipathy, born of centuries of a highly idiosyncratic history, to the ideal of the unitary, centralized, national state, and a willingness to consider the claims of religion as a determining factor in political affairs.

Such feelings were apt on occasions to give an appearance of inconsistency and ambiguity to the behaviour of politicians in the Rhine valley. Thus Eugen Ricklin, the Alsatian autonomist who led the opposition to the German military authorities before the First World War, after the war founded a newspaper and a Home Rule League to oppose the centralizing policy of the French and to demand complete autonomy within the French state. Görres, during the Napoleonic wars, went through a similar evolution, though in an opposite direction, in first welcoming the French invaders as the defenders of Rhineland autonomy and then appealing to German patriotism as a means of protection from the French; in both cases regional rights and traditions were regarded as of greater importance than the claims of nationalism, whether French or German.

The war of 1914–18 once again allowed the Germans to exploit their bridgehead on the left bank of the Rhine to execute a rapid and sweeping advance into Flanders and Northern France, with an initial weight and impetus which almost, but not quite, enabled them to repeat the triumph of 1870. Though they failed to reach their objective, their advance gave them the advantage of fighting the war for four years on French soil and of forcing the French and their allies to undertake repeated and enormously costly offensives under conditions which were all in favour of the defence. In 1914–18, as in 1870, command of the Rhine crossings leading to the invasion routes into France gave the strategic initiative to the Germans, and not until their own resources were exhausted did they lose the benefit of their initial advantage.

It was natural therefore that the first objective of the Allies after the armistice was to occupy the left bank of the Rhine, and, on its right bank, Cologne, Coblenz and Mainz. For France especially the most important of all war aims was to secure permanent control both of the left bank and of bridgeheads on the right bank which would secure the vital crossings over the river. Yet even her aims did not extend to annexation; such an objective was unattainable in the political atmosphere of 1918, when the sacred principle of nationality was accepted by both victors and vanquished as the basis of a just and permanent peace. France did indeed secure the return of the lost provinces of Alsace and Lorraine, but in the decisive strategic area of the Rhineland her hopes were limited to establishing a neutral, autonomous state, under French influence and liberated from domination by Berlin.

Such hopes may seem now to have been entirely illusory. In her attempt to establish an independent Rhineland state, which was a reversion to the policy she pursued in the eighteenth century, France received neither sympathy nor support from her allies, who believed both that the principle of nationality prohibited any territorial changes in an area that was German by race and by language, and that the provisions of the Treaty of Versailles and of the Covenant of the League of Nations were a sufficient guarantee of France's security. France, invaded twice in less than fifty years, was not unnaturally dissatisfied with assurances that in the long run rested on nothing stronger than the good faith both of her allies and of her defeated enemy and once again tried to draw the Rhineland within the orbit of her influence.

In the circumstances which followed the armistice of 1918 such a policy was not entirely without prospects. An independent, or autonomous, Rhineland state would have had behind it a long historical tradition and strong feelings of local patriotism, even though, in the years since 1870, these had been diluted by a large incursion of industrial workers from north Germany, who were attracted by the industrial expansion that had taken place in the Rhine Province. When the Allies entered the Rhineland they were welcomed as the representatives of law and order, at a time when the German state appeared to be disintegrating, and as a protection against the dangers of civil war as a result of the revolution in Berlin. The separatist movement in the Rhineland, with French support, raised the cry of *Los von Berlin* (Away from Berlin) and demanded the establishment of a *droit Rhenane*, a constitutional status for the Rhineland that would guarantee its right to self-government. At Coblenz, Mainz, Trier, Speyer, Wiesbaden and Aachen there were popular demonstrations in favour of a Rhineland republic; the French lent their support to the separatist leader Dr Dorten, who demanded autonomy for a Rhineland state, which would include Nassau, Rhein-Hesse and the Palatinate, and with its capital at Coblenz.

The separatist movement in the Rhineland was based on a complex of feelings and attitudes which were hostile to government from Berlin; they were intensified by the anti-clerical policy of the Socialist government of the Reich, But they also reflected the shock of defeat, the revolutionary turmoil that swept Germany at the end of the war, the prestige of the victorious Allies and the decline in the authority of the central Reich government, which was simultaneously threatened by separatist movements in Bavaria, under Kurt Eisner, in Saxony under Fleisner, and even in the tiny principality of Birkenfeld; but whereas separatism in Bavaria and in Saxony was under Communist and Left-wing Socialist leadership, in the Rhineland it was essentially Conservative and Catholic.

The claims of increased local autonomy, if not of complete independence, seemed to be supported by the new Weimar Constitution which stipulated that 'the division of the empire into separate states should have regard as much as possible to the will of the populations concerned and to the maximum freedom of their peoples in economic and cultural affairs,' and gave grounds for hoping that the new Germany would have a federalist character. In fact, the Socialist government of the Reich pursued the policy of centralization even further than the imperial Government had done and appeared to justify Spengler's paradox in his *Preussentum und Socialismus* that Socialism was the true heir of the Hohenzollerns. In Gustav Noske Weimar found a Socialist Minister of Defence who was as determined to maintain the unity and territorial integrity of the Reich as any pan-German; on the basis of a secret understanding with the Reichswehr, he ruthlessly suppressed the separatist movements in the Rhineland, in Saxony and Bavaria. Risings in favour of autonomy for the Rhineland were suppressed at Kaiserslautern, Dürckheim and Pirmasens with a severity which justified the French in describing them as *les Vêpres Rhenanes*.

The year 1923 indeed may be said to have seen the end of separatism in the Rhineland. The sovereignty of the Reich on the left bank of the river had been preserved for Germany by the Weimar Republic, which henceforward pursued a policy of centralization which left no room for separatism or federalism. Moreover, the French themselves helped to give the final blow to separatism in the Rhineland; the occupation of the Ruhr by Franco-Belgian forces in 1923, in an effort to compel Germany to meet her reparations payments, provoked a patriotic reaction of which, in the long run, the only beneficiaries were the most extreme forms of German nationalism. It is a curious by-product of the Franco-German conflict in the Ruhr that the only modern martyr of the Rhine, a region so rich in saints and martyrs, was the degenerate Loe Schlageter who was later to be canonized by the National Socialist movement.

Thus the settlement of Versailles neither restored France's position on the Rhine nor advanced the Rhineland's claims to autonomy. And it is significant, as evidence that such claims were in fact incompatible with the nature of either the French or the German state, that while France, for reasons of foreign policy, supported Rhineland separatism against Germany, in her own recovered provinces of Alsace-Lorraine she firmly repressed federalist tendencies, based on demands for a special status within the framework of the French Republic. In 1911, the Germans had conferred on Alsace-Lorraine a constitution which gave the region a parliament of its own; in 1918, for the period of eleven days which elapsed between the withdrawal of the German garrison and the arrival of French troops, it had exercised all the legislative and executive powers of a sovereign government, under the name of the National Council of Alsace-Lorraine. Its independence was short lived. Clemenceau immediately applied a policy of rigid centralization, which was strongly resisted by the population; and though Millerand, who was dispatched to Strasbourg by Clemenceau in an effort to pacify popular discontent, attempted to restore local forms of administration and self-government, he gave up the task halfway in order to become first Prime Minister and then President of the Republic. Alsace-Lorraine became an integral part of France like any other, though this in no way corresponded to its special status as a French outpost on the Rhine, profoundly attached to France but largely German by race and by language. 'The majority of Alsatians,' said the German critic, Ernst Robert Curtius, 'have both a French conception of the state and a German conception of the nation, which the Germans find great difficulty in understanding and the French even more.' In varying degrees, this statement might be held to apply to the people of the Rhine valley as a whole, and to explain why in the age of nationalism they never found themselves wholly at their ease either within the German or the French state.

If the Treaty of Versailles did not satisfy the demands of either separatism or federalism on the Rhine, neither did it satisfy French claims to security. The Treaty gave the Allies the right to occupy the left bank of the river, with bridgeheads on the right bank, for a period of fifteen years, as a guarantee that Germany would fulfil the terms of the Treaty; evacuation of the occupied zone was to be carried out by stages, to be completed in 1935. The occupation was envisaged as a purely military operation, carried out with the minimum of force, which was not intended permanently to impair or diminish German sovereignty on the Rhine. 'I am accused of occupying a country' said Foch. 'That is completely untrue. I am engaged in occupying the crossings of the Rhine, which requires very small forces.' When evacuation was completed the left bank of the Rhine was to remain a demilitarized zone. The future of the Saar territory was to be determined by a plebiscite.

None of these measures proved sufficient to guard France against the dangers of German control of the left bank of the river. The evacuation of the Rhineland was completed five years in advance of the timetable provided for by the Treaty, and in June 1930 the French marched out of Mainz and Wiesbaden; in the previous year Foch had uttered a last despairing cry against the dangers involved, 'There is no exaggeration in saying that the evacuation of the Rhineland, if unfortunately it were to take place tomorrow, will leave France without a frontier and without an army. . . . To consider evacuating the Rhineland would truly be a crime against the Fatherland.'

Events confirmed Foch's prediction. In the year that the Rhineland was evacuated, the Germans returned 107 National Socialists to the Reichstag, and thereafter Germany was subjected to the pressure of a steadily mounting campaign of propaganda combined with terror designed to create the highest possible degree of national unity in preparation for war. In 1935, the plebiscite in the Saar territory produced a majority for Hitler of 90.7% of the electorate. In 1936, Hitler occupied the demilitarized zone on the left bank of the Rhine, without any effective opposition being offered by the Western powers, and thereby secured the indispensable condition for mounting a renewed invasion of France.

It is worth noticing that, while National Socialism triumphed in Germany, and while the nation as a whole applauded every step which brought Hitler nearer to complete and absolute power, the Rhineland tended to be unenthusiastic. Indeed it could be said that support for Hitler tended to fall as one travelled from east to west across Germany. In the plebiscite of 19 August 1934, which made Hitler head of the German state in succession to President Hindenburg, the proportion of negative votes rose from 4% in Königsberg, in East Prussia, to 25% in Cologne and to more than 40% in Aachen (50,000 votes against 74,000). It must be added that the Rhineland produced some of Hitler's closest associates, such as Goebbels, Ribbentrop, Ley, Frick and Bürckel.

The significant proportion of hostile votes in the Rhineland may be considered a reflection of political attitudes and tendencies which had been deeply rooted there for centuries, to all of which National Socialism stood in complete contradiction. But opposition to Hitler was no more effective on the Rhine than elsewhere. The Catholic Centre Party, especially, which was its most characteristic contribution to the politics of the Reich, proved notably ineffectual in combating the combination of propaganda, terror, nationalist appeal and political chicanery by which Hitler fought his way to power. It was at the house of a Rhineland banker, Schröder, at a meeting engineered by a member of the Centre party, Papen, that Hitler arrived at the agreement with the Conservative leader Hugenberg which was one of the decisive steps in his conquest of power. And it was from Rhineland industrialists that he received the first substantial financial contributions to his party funds, which enabled him to finance the Nationalist Socialist movement while he was still in opposition.

Hitler's remilitarization of the Rhineland once again gave Germany the opportunity to launch an invasion of France, and indeed with such force and violence that even the triumph of 1870 was surpassed. The Maginot line, which the French had built as a kind of artificial substitute for the water barrier of the

Rhine, proved to be wholly ineffective; indeed, it merely intensified the defensive mentality of the French without offering any serious obstacle to the German advance. The development of operations in the west once again illustrated the advantage accruing to an invader from the east who commanded the Rhine crossings and a bridgehead on the left bank which allowed his troops to exploit the routes running west from them into the Low Countries and Northern France.

From Cologne to Pannerden the vital crossings of the Rhine, at Cologne, Düsseldorf, Duisburg, Wesel and Emmerich all lay within German territory; to advance west the invasion forces required only to secure the crossings of the Meuse between Graves and Liège. In Holland, the main route from Bremen to Antwerp crossed the Waal and the Lek, within a distance of twenty miles of each other, at Arnhem and Nijmwegen, and the Meuse at Graves. This route passed by Eindhoven, and beyond Antwerp led to Ghent and Lille. To the south, along the edge of the Eifel, the invasion route led from Cologne via Aachen, Liège and Namur to Charleroi; crossing the Rhine at Cologne, and the Meuse at Maastricht, it followed the valley of the Meuse and the Sambre to the area formed by the sources of the Sambre, the Scheldt, the Somme and the Oise which commands the routes to the Channel and to Paris. Between these two routes lay a third which led from the Rhine crossings at Wesel, Duisburg and Düsseldorf across the Meuse at Venlo and Roermond to Belgium.

The initial stages of the German campaign in the west in 1940 was essentially a battle of river crossings. By the 10th of May, the Germans had crossed the Meuse, advanced along the arms of the Rhine into Holland and within four days had defeated the Dutch army and advanced across Belgium to the frontiers of France. The speed of the German advance was a demonstration that, west of the Rhine, there is no effective natural barrier against an invader from the east. In addition, any invader from the east possesses the logistical advantage of being able to supply his forces across the Rhine by the shortest possible routes; in the case of the Germans, the crossings of the Rhine led directly from their main industrial base in the Ruhr. When the tide of battle turned, and the Allied armies landed in Normandy in June 1944, it was equally demonstrated that, while the crossings of the Rhine gave an immense advantage to an invader from the east, they gave an equal advantage in defence against an invader from the west. As the Allies advanced from Normandy, their lines of supply became increasingly extended, and the protracted German defence of Antwerp and the mouths of the Rhine denied them the use of short sea routes from their main base in the United Kingdom. The logistical problem was further complicated by the Allied decision to advance along the whole length of their front instead of concentrating on a single thrust into the heart of Germany. While it took the Germans four days to reach the French frontier in Belgium after crossing the Meuse, it took the Allies four months to reach the Rhine in Holland; the battle of the Rhine itself took seven months, from the failure of Field-Marshal Montgomery's attempt to seize Arnhem in September 1944 to the capitulation of Field-Marshal Model's armies in the Ruhr, on 18 April 1945.

The final objective of the Allied campaign in the west in 1944–45 was to cross the Rhine and strike into the industrial heart of Germany in the Ruhr. To achieve this objective took in all nine months, from the landing in Normandy on 6 June 1944 until General Hodges' troops crossed the river at Remagen on 7 March 1945; it required the concentrated action of five Allied armies, with overwhelming air superiority, which were engaged in hard and continuous fighting for the whole of the five months that elapsed after they reached the Rhine at Strasbourg in November 1944. This may be compared with the three days which it took the Germans to cross the Meuse at Sedan in 1940.

In the battles in the west in 1940 and 1944–45 the Germans derived an immense strategical advantage from their command of the Rhine crossings and of a bridgehead on its left bank. In the post-war occupation of Germany, and in the foundation of the German Federal Republic the Western Powers recognized, as they did not in 1918, that control of a wide bridgehead on the right bank of the Rhine, either under Allied occupation, or in the hands of a friendly German state, was indispensable to the defence of western Europe. Equally, it was an object of Allied policy that any German state controlling the Rhine and the approaches to it should have a federal constitution in which the powers of the federal state should be strong enough to provide a restraint upon the central government.

In this sense it can be said that the post-war settlement of Germany at length decided the problem of the Rhine to the advantage of the Western Powers. It could also be said that the post-war settlement in West Germany was fundamentally in harmony with the long historical traditions and the age-old aspirations of the people of the Rhine valley. It would not be an exaggeration to describe the German Federal Republic as essentially a Rhineland state, conservative, Catholic and federalist, and with its industrial power concentrated on the banks of the Rhine. The partition of Germany has realized, to an extent that few could ever have forseen, the separatist cry of *Los von Berlin*, and the destruction of Prussia has removed, for the forseeable future, fears that the Rhine can ever again be used to mount a German invasion from the east. From the point of view of western Europe as a whole, including West Germany, the Federal Republic serves precisely as that defensive barrier and bridgehead along the right bank of the Rhine which was for so long the object of French policy.

But one can say also that the post-war settlement has realized the historical tradition of the Rhine valley in another and deeper sense. The development of the atomic bomb and the H-bomb, and the revolution in military strategy and tactics which it has inspired, has no doubt reduced the strategic significance of the Rhine, though as long as war remains a reality or a possibility it will remain one of the decisive military factors in Europe. But the post-war development of the European Economic Community depends essentially on the intimate and continuous collaboration and friendship of France and Germany, and in the task of creating such a community the Rhine valley has a function for which it is uniquely equipped by geography, by history and the temperament and age-old interests of its peoples.

In the kind of Europe which is developing out of the European

Economic Community, it is likely that the Rhine will have a future which will be even greater than its past. For in the past, especially in the more recent past, it has often been the tragic function of the river to become a battle ground for the most intense national rivalries and ambitions; the logical end of this process was the terrible devastation which the Rhine valley suffered during the Second World War. In a new Europe it should be the destiny of the Rhine rather to fulfil its natural function of a great river uniting all the peoples which adjoin its banks, politically, commercially and culturally, and it is only under the conditions of a united Europe that it can fully perform this function. The Rhine is essentially a European river, and part of its immense fascination is precisely the images of the European past which are reflected in its waters; today, as a European river, its happiness and prosperity coincide with those of Europe itself.

Index